Choosing Well

Choosing Well

The Good, the Bad, and the Trivial

CHRISOULA ANDREOU

OXFORD
UNIVERSITY PRESS

OXFORD
UNIVERSITY PRESS

Oxford University Press is a department of the University of Oxford. It furthers
the University's objective of excellence in research, scholarship, and education
by publishing worldwide. Oxford is a registered trade mark of Oxford University
Press in the UK and certain other countries.

Published in the United States of America by Oxford University Press
198 Madison Avenue, New York, NY 10016, United States of America.

Library of Congress Cataloging-in-Publication Data
Names: Andreou, Chrisoula, author.
Title: Choosing well : the good, the bad, and the trivial / Chrisoula Andreou.
Description: First. | New York, NY. United States of America : Oxford
University Press, 2023. | Includes bibliographical references and index.
Identifiers: LCCN 2022029843 (print) | LCCN 2022029844 (ebook) |
ISBN 9780197584132 (hardback) | ISBN 9780197584156 (epub)
Subjects: LCSH: Choice (Psychology) | Decision making.
Classification: LCC BF611 .A535 2022 (print) | LCC BF611 (ebook) |
DDC 153.8/3—dc23/eng/20220725
LC record available at https://lccn.loc.gov/2022029843
LC ebook record available at https://lccn.loc.gov/2022029844

DOI: 10.1093/oso/9780197584132.001.0001

1 3 5 7 9 8 6 4 2

Printed by Integrated Books International, United States of America

For my parents, Ritsa and Steve Andreou, with love, gratitude, and admiration.

Contents

Preface

Self-defeating behavior and the frustration it can cause constitute a deep and rich area of philosophical inquiry. This book synthesizes and incorporates, in part or with some modifications, a variety of my contributions, published over many years, on the demands of effective decision-making in the face of challenging choice situations that generate disorderly preferences and threaten to prompt self-defeating patterns of choice. The result is a unified, extended study of the role of rationality in accommodating certain well-grounded but disorderly preference structures while protecting us from associated self-defeating patterns of choice.

The book's introduction, first chapter, and conclusion include selections (sometimes paraphrased or modified as needed to fit my current purposes) from "Environmental Damage and the Puzzle of the Self-Torturer" (*Philosophy & Public Affairs*, 2006a), "Empowering Rationality" (*American Philosophical Quarterly*, 2020a), "There Are Preferences and Then There Are Preferences" (*Economics and the Mind*, 2007a), "Rationality, Regret, and Choice over Time" (*Routledge Handbook of Practical Reason*, 2020b), "Dynamic Choice" (*Stanford Encyclopedia of Philosophy*, 2017), "Sweating the Small Stuff" (*Psychology Today* [online], 2010), and from several of the papers mentioned below in connection with later chapters in the book. Chapter 2 is a modified version of "Self-Defeating Self-Governance" (*Philosophical Issues*, 2012). (As in other chapters, the modifications allowed the chapter to figure as part of a larger integrated whole and to be refined in light of relatively recent feedback.) Chapter 3 combines modified versions of "The Real Puzzle of the Self-Torturer" (*Canadian Journal of*

Philosophy, 2015a) and "Cashing Out the Money-Pump Argument" (*Philosophical Studies*, 2016). Chapter 4 combines a modified version of "Parity, Comparability, and Choice" (*Journal of Philosophy*, 2015b) with modified selections from "Parity without Imprecise Equality" (*Value Incommensurability*, 2022). Chapter 5 is a modified version of "Incomparability and the Huge-Improvement Arguments" (*American Philosophical Quarterly*, 2021). Chapter 6 combines a modified version of "Better Than" (*Philosophical Studies*, 2019a) with modified selections from "In a Different League" (*Derek Parfit's Reasons and Persons*, 2020c). Chapter 7 is a modified version of "Temptation, Resolutions, and Regret" (*Inquiry*, 2014a). And Chapter 8 is a modified version of "Regret, Sub-Optimality, and Vagueness" (*Vagueness and Rationality in Language Use and Cognition*, 2019b). The book's title is drawn from titles I've used for other pieces, including the title of my *Psychology Today* blog "Choosing Well: The Good, the Bad, and the Negligible" (2010), and the titles of my articles "Choosing Well: Value Pluralism and Patterns of Choice" (*New Waves in Ethics*, 2011) and "The Good, the Bad, and the Trivial" (*Philosophical Studies*, 2014).

My thanks to colleagues who provided helpful feedback on these papers or on their integration into the larger, systematic whole that turned into this book. I received a slew of thought-provoking comments from the multiple editors and anonymous referees of individually published papers, audience members at various venues at which the main ideas that made it into the book were presented, and the following individuals: Arif Ahmed, George Ainslie, Jack Anderson, Henrik Andersson, Kenneth Arrow, Rima Basu, Kevin Baum, Idil Boran, Luc Bovens, Michael Bratman, Talbot Brewer, Donald Bruckner, John Brunero, Mark Budolfson, Sarah Buss, Krister Bykvist, Ruth Chang, Matt Cox, Ben Crowe, Richard Dietz, Nives Dolšak, Tom Dougherty, Ben Eggleston, Christoph Fehige, Luca Ferrero, Leslie Francis, Matthew Frise, Robert Frodeman, Stephen Gardiner, Olav Gjelsvik, Preston Greene, Robert Goldberg, Johan Gustafsson, Ian Hamilton, Joseph Heath, Richard Holton,

Dale Jamieson, Dan Lassiter, Hannah Love, Christoph Lumer, Duncan MacIntosh, Chaone Mallory, Edward McClennen, Elijah Millgram, Barbara Montero, Michael Morreau, Adam Morton, Julia Nefsky, Shaun Nichols, Stephan Padel, Derek Parfit, Sarah Paul, Douglas Portmore, Theron Pummer, Wlodek Rabinowicz, Andrew Reisner, Adam Riggio, Holmes Rolston III, Don Ross, Mauro Rossi, Andrea Sauchelli, Jonah Schupbach, Walter Sinnott-Armstrong, Will Small, Jacob Stegenga, Sarah Stroud, Jim Tabery, Christine Tappolet, Larry Temkin, Sergio Tenenbaum, Mariam Thalos, Johanna Thoma, Manuel Utset, Peter Vallentyne, Ralph Wedgwood, Mark D. White, Mike White, Nick White, Gideon Yaffe, and Chris Zarpentine. I am especially indebted to Michael Bratman, Ruth Chang, Elijah Millgram, Michael Morreau, Douglas Portmore, Wlodek Rabinowicz, Sarah Stroud, Christine Tappolet, Larry Temkin, Sergio Tenenbaum, Mariam Thalos, and Mike White for their recurring involvement. Over the years during which I developed the ideas in this book, I benefited from support from the University of Utah, the College of Humanities at the University of Utah, the Tanner Humanities Center, the Sterling M. McMurrin Award, the Charles H. Monson Esteemed Faculty Award, and from institutions, organization, or agencies that invited me to present my work. My thanks also to Valéry Giroux, who provided extremely helpful organizational support during my multiple visits to CRE, the *Centre de Recherche en Éthique*, in Montreal. Last but not least, I am extremely grateful for the constant personal support provided by my family, Mike White and Kaemon Andreou-White. Note that, to avoid repetition, acknowledgments provided in this preface will generally not be included within the text as well.

Finally, let me flag that, when using a pronoun to refer to a generic agent, and when using pronouns in illustrations featuring a specific fictitious agent, I use one of "she," "he," or the nonbinary singular "they" (i.e., the "they" that refers to a nonbinary person), rather than the unwieldy "she, he, or they," recognizing, of course, that none of these terms figures as the personal (sometimes referred to as "preferred") pronoun of all agents or as a generally accepted gender-neutral singular pronoun. Note that, given my limited knowledge concerning the variety of practical and theoretical complications regarding distributing the different pronouns, I certainly do not mean to suggest that the distribution in this manuscript follows some approach that is free of pitfalls or that there is no better way of departing from certain familiar approaches wherein nonbinary persons do not appear at all. It is perhaps worth mentioning that the distribution is not indicative of current estimates regarding the proportion of individuals who identify as nonbinary, which appears to be relatively small. It is, however, in a way, more consonant with such estimates than certain alternative distributions that might be considered (such as, for example, a distribution involving a default that minimizes current use of the historically overrepresented "he" in favor of, say, alternating, whenever practicable, between "she" and the nonbinary singular "they"). The greater consonance may be for better or for worse, depending on a proper assessment of the relative advantages and pitfalls of different approaches. As with other aspects of the book, I welcome as many thoughtful comments as I am lucky to receive.

Introduction

Choosing well can be quite the challenge and, in many cases, seemingly modest claims paper over philosophically interesting complications. Consider, for instance, the idea that one should not "sweat the small stuff" or, more formally, that one should treat trivial effects as trivial. This seems like solid, or at worst superfluous, advice, but, when you think about it, not sweating the small stuff can be a recipe for disaster. Why? Because big stuff is made of small stuff and, presumably, we should sweat the big stuff, which suggests that we really should sweat the small stuff after all. Consider some examples familiar from everyday life on the many ways in which we often voluntarily inch toward terrible results. We eat too much, save too little, and wreak havoc on the environment; but, in many cases, each step toward unhealthy weight gain, destitution, and environmental destruction seems trivial in terms of making things worse than they are. Perhaps, paradoxically, it does not make sense to consistently treat trivial effects as trivial. One thing that is clear is that choosing well and theorizing about choosing well can be quite tricky. To put the point more positively, getting a handle on what choosing well involves can be of great philosophical and practical import.

This book focuses on the challenges associated with effective choice over time. Its contributions are meant to be of both theoretical and practical interest, and indeed to illustrate the power of theoretical models in illuminating debate about practical problems. I focus, in particular, on the challenges raised by *cyclic preferences* and by *preference gaps*. One's preferences with respect to a set of options count as cyclic when one cannot rank the options from

Choosing Well. Chrisoula Andreou, Oxford University Press. © Oxford University Press 2023.
DOI: 10.1093/oso/9780197584132.003.0001

Figure I.1 Read "Y< X" as "X is preferred to Y."

most preferred to least preferred because one's preferences form a loop, as, for example, in Figure I.1. To take an all-too-familiar case of cyclic preferences, an agent may prefer, on each day $\{d_0, d_1, d_2, \ldots, d_{1000}\}$, to put off dieting for just one more day, but also prefer starting to diet at d_0 over starting to diet at d_{1000}. Preference gaps also preclude the agent neatly ordering the available options from most preferred to least preferred, even allowing for ties, since, insofar as a set of preferences include gaps, not every option is ranked in relation to every other option (not even as exactly equally favored). An agent might, for example, find themselves unable to rank pursuing a particular artistic activity and pursuing a particular athletic activity because they see the options as neither one better than the other nor exactly equally good.[1] Although cyclic preferences and preference gaps often arise quite naturally, they make the agent susceptible to self-defeating patterns of choice in which the agent is drawn into taking each of a series of steps that collectively lead the agent to a result that they deem unacceptable. Consider, for example, that in the diet case, the agent might end up binging for 1,000 days in a row, after repeatedly deciding to put off dieting for one more day. In the artistic versus athletic activities case, the agent might, given the

---

[1] See the preface regarding the replacement of "she, he, or they" with one of these singular personal (sometimes referred to as "preferred") pronouns, in this particular case "they." I will not continue flagging instances in which "she, he, or they" is replaced with one of "she," "he," or "they."

choice between the two activities, start pursing one option but then waver and incur a small cost to switch to pursuing the other option, which was available to the agent before without the extra cost.

My guiding questions in this book are the following: What is an agent to do if she finds herself with *cyclic preferences* or with *preference gaps*? Is an agent with such preferences necessarily irrational? In my view, the answer to the latter question is "no"; rationality does not invariably prohibit disorderly preferences, but it does (to get back to the first question) prompt us to proceed with caution and with a readiness to show restraint, based on an awareness of larger dynamics, when our preferences are disorderly. Theories of rational choice often dismiss or abstract away from the sorts of disorderly preferences that I focus on. They assume that rational agents can and should have neat preferences over their options; but this assumption is problematic. As I will explain, rationality can validate certain disorderly preference structures while also protecting us from self-defeating patterns of choice.

Ultimately, my reasoning regarding cyclic preferences and preference gaps leads me to a revisionary way of understanding instrumental rationality. In particular, my reasoning supports the conclusion that the subjective appraisal responses to which instrumental rationality is accountable go beyond the appraisal responses captured by an agent's preferences (which are the only subjective appraisal responses recognized by standard conceptions of instrumental rationality); they also include what I call *categorial subjective appraisal responses*. Recognition of these additional responses is important for properly understanding the major pitfall associated with disorderly preferences and for seeing how it can be averted.

The book is organized as follows: In Chapter 1, I focus first on the requirement, in rational choice theory, that an agent's preferences be *acyclic* (i.e., non-cyclic). It is commonly acknowledged that preferences can include preference cycles (or loops). Relatedly, the requirements of rational choice theory are not normally understood as describing or defining preferences but instead as either rational requirements on preferences or else as conditions that preferences must satisfy for rationality to be able to provide an agent with guidance. The requirement of acyclicity is often defended as a requirement of rationality based on the *money-pump argument*, which suggests that an agent with cyclic preferences is susceptible to self-defeating patterns of choice, wherein following her preferences leads her to incur a sure loss. More specifically, the argument suggests that an agent with cyclic preferences is susceptible to serving as a money pump wherein the agent repeatedly incurs a small cost to upgrade relative to her preferences, and, because her preferences are cyclic, ends up with the same option she began with, but with less money. After reviewing the money-pump argument, I consider a defense of the possibility of rationally cyclic preferences. In particular, I focus on cases in which cyclic preferences seem perfectly appropriate and on reasons for thinking that cyclic preferences can be generated by defensible ways of comparing alternatives. I also revisit the money-pump argument and suggest that there is room for reinterpreting it so that it figures not as an argument against the rational permissibility of cyclic preferences, but instead as an argument against the idea that a rational agent is invariably guided by her preferences. Preferences will, I assume, often be revealed in choice. But this is not inevitably the case, since there are complications involving, for instance, habits, non-deliberative follow-through on prior plans, and/or the recognition of a conflict between acting on some of one's preferences and doing justice to one's categorial subjective appraisal responses (as discussed in Chapter 3), that can prompt an agent to act contrary to her preferences.

Next, I focus on the requirement, in rational choice theory, that an agent's preferences be *complete*. According to the requirement of completeness, an agent's preferences must be such that for all options X and Y, the agent prefers X to Y, or prefers Y to X, or is indifferent between X and Y. This precludes preference gaps wherein two options are not ranked by the agent's preferences (not even as exactly equally favored). As with cyclic preferences, incomplete preferences, although they can raise challenges for the agent, sometimes arise quite naturally. I consider a defense of the rational permissibility of incomplete preferences in terms of the possibility of *incommensurable alternatives*, understood as alternatives that are neither one better than the other (at least not determinately so), nor exactly equally good. The possibility of incommensurable alternatives helps make sense of incomplete preferences even apart from the fact that having preferences over all possible options seems beyond our capacities as agents with limited mental resources. Where two options are neither one better than the other, nor exactly equally good, a preference gap between them seems perfectly appropriate.

The possibility of incommensurable alternatives is generally supported via an appeal to cases that fit the *small-improvement argument*. According to this argument, there are cases in which A is not better than B, B is not better than A, and A+ (a slightly improved version of A) is better than A but not better than B. Given the plausible assumption that if two options are exactly equally good, then a further option that is better than one of the options will be better than the other option as well—an assumption that is not impacted by my reasoning about rationally cyclic preferences if, as I argue in Chapter 6, "better than" can and should be understood as acyclic even if "is rationally preferred to" is not—it follows that, in addition to not being one better than the other, A and B are not exactly equally good either. In light of what I see as a particularly compelling small-improvement scenario, I am led, as in the first part of Chapter 1, to the idea that rationality sometimes requires not that our preferences be neat and orderly, but instead that we proceed with caution and with an awareness of larger dynamics when our preferences are disorderly.

In Chapter 2, I argue that the sort of self-defeating patterns of choice that agents with cyclic and incomplete preferences must guard against is particularly interesting because it cannot be explained in terms of the self losing control over behavior. Rather, things go badly even though the self remains at the helm (and is informed about the consequences of each option). It might seem as though informed behavior cannot be both self-defeating and self-governed. Consider the following line of reasoning (which I have set apart and slightly indented so that its scope is clear—an arrangement that will occur repeatedly without further flagging):

> If one's behavior is self-governed, it is governed by values and commitments with which one identifies and which one does not find alien; and so, one's behavior is true to oneself. Assuming it is based on an awareness of the consequences of each choice one makes, behavior that is true to oneself does not also defeat this same self, and so self-governed behavior is not self-defeating.

We are thus left with a dilemma that seems to undermine the possibility of informed self-defeating behavior. On the one hand, given that self-defeat involves being defeated by oneself, if some behavior is not self-governed, it cannot be self-defeating. On the other hand, given that self-governance involves being true to oneself, if some behavior is self-governed, it cannot, assuming it is informed, be self-defeating. So, it seems that, if informed, neither self-governed behavior nor behavior that is not self-governed can be self-defeating.

One response to this dilemma is to grant that self-defeating behavior, understood as behavior involving the defeat of one's self by one's self—where the self in question is defined, roughly speaking, in terms of one's commitments and values—is indeed impossible, but to stress that in a looser sense, wherein self-defeat involves the defeat of one's self by desires and behaviors that one disowns despite recognizing them as in some sense one's own, self-defeating behavior is possible. In this weaker sense, the classic case of the unwilling addict, who persistently disowns her desire for drugs even as she persistently seeks out drugs, is a case of self-defeating behavior. My focus, however, is on vindicating the possibility of behavior that is self-defeating in a stronger sense—a sense in which the desires and behaviors that are defeating one's self are ones with which one identifies. I thus move away from the classic case of the unwilling addict and consider two other types of cases in which it is tempting to say that the agent's behavior is self-defeating. The first case, which involves preference reversals, gets us closer than the classic case of the unwilling addict to a case of strictly self-defeating behavior. The second case, which involves cyclic preferences, arguably gets us all the way there. After considering the second case, I turn to interesting complications raised by cases involving incommensurable alternatives. I conclude by explaining the implications of the possibility of self-defeating self-governance for instrumental rationality.

In Chapter 3, I first raise and solve a puzzle about the emerging conception of instrumental rationality, according to which instrumental rationality allows for certain forms of disorderliness but requires that one proceed with caution and sometimes show restraint so as to avoid ending up realizing a self-defeating pattern of choice. In a nutshell, the puzzle can be described as follows: If showing restraint (from the point of view of instrumental rationality) is a matter of settling on a dispreferred option, and realizing a self-defeating pattern of choice is a matter of realizing a dispreferred option, then showing restraint so as to avoid ending up realizing a self-defeating pattern of choice amounts to settling on a dispreferred option so as to avoid realizing a dispreferred option, which doesn't make sense.

I solve this puzzle by distinguishing between *relational subjective appraisal responses* and *categorial subjective appraisal responses*, and interpreting these responses as figuring, in human psychology, as two distinct kinds of responses. Relational subjective appraisal responses rank options in relation to one another; it is these appraisal responses that are captured by the agent's preferences. (Note that I'll be loosely describing the favoring of one option in a pair as the ranking of that option over the other—even when no ranking of all the options is to be had because the agent's preferences are cyclic. If my use of "ranking" seems too loose, it can be eliminated by the reader via appropriate substitutions.) By contrast, categorial subjective appraisal responses place options in categories, such as, for example, "great" or "terrible." While instrumental rationality is standardly understood as accountable to only relational subjective appraisal responses, I argue that it is also accountable to categorial subjective appraisal responses. If this is right, then we can make sense of the idea that, in cases involving rationally cyclic preferences, instrumental rationality sometimes calls for showing restraint so as to avoid ending up realizing a self-defeating pattern of choice. For, when preferences are rationally cyclic, we can interpret "showing restraint" as "settling on a dispreferred option" and interpret the demand that one avoid realizing a self-defeating pattern of choice as requiring (perhaps among other things) *not* that one avoid realizing a dispreferred option, since that is not possible, but that one avoid ending up in an unnecessarily low appraisal category (e.g., ending up with a terrible option when great options are available).

In the last section of Chapter 3, I raise and solve a similar puzzle regarding the money-pump argument. The puzzle is as follows: According to a prominent interpretation of the money-pump argument, the argument is supposed to show that cyclic preferences are irrational by showing that following one's cyclic preferences can lead one to a dispreferred alternative. But then the argument is grounded in the *assumption* that it is irrational to make choices that lead one to a dispreferred alternative; and, as I explain, this assumption arguably begs the question against someone who thinks rational preference cycles are possible. The assumption that it is irrational to make choices that lead one to a dispreferred alternative is also problematic in relation to the reinterpretation of the money-pump argument presented in Chapter 1, which allows for rationally cyclic preferences and casts the threat of being money pumped as undermining the idea that a rational agent will invariably act on her preferences. For, if one allows for rationally cyclic preferences, then one must grant that even a rational agent can be in a position where she must settle on a dispreferred alternative. But then it cannot be assumed that it is irrational to make choices that lead one to a dispreferred alternative. The solution is to see the money-pump argument as relying on an assumption that is common ground between opponents and defenders of rationally cyclic preferences, namely the assumption that rationality requires one to avoid any alternative A- that is exactly the same as some other available alternative A except for one disadvantageous difference. Interpreted in this way, the argument is reestablished as forcefully suggesting that either rational preferences cannot be cyclic or rational agents do not invariably follow their preferences.

In Chapter 4, I return to the distinction between relational and categorial appraisal responses and use it to illuminate the possibility of incommensurable alternatives and incomplete preferences. In particular, I show that, insofar as we have both categorial appraisal responses and relational appraisal responses, we should expect there to be many cases of parity in which the options are "in the same league" or "in the same neighborhood" but not comparable as one better than the other or as exactly equally good (relative to what matters in the case at hand). To begin with, I consider cases in which all that matters in the case at hand is the current appeal to the agent of each option. In such cases, all that is relevant is the agent's subjective appraisal responses. But relational subjective appraisal responses on the part of an agent will often be limited to cases in which the options are quite similar to one another (as with A and A+, where A+ is a slightly improved version of A) or else different enough to elicit different categorial responses. In cases where the agent has the same categorial subjective appraisal response to two options that are quite different from one another (e.g., both options are excellent), the agent may find herself with no relational subjective appraisal response at all. Her preferences will thus be incomplete and not because she is missing some pertinent information, since, by hypothesis, the matter is purely subjective. After considering some objections to my position, I show how it can be built on to illuminate cases of parity even when what matters is not purely subjective.

Significantly, my appeal to categorial appraisal responses can help explain how two options that are neither one better than the other nor exactly equally good can be on a par (in terms of their overall value relative to what matters in the case at hand) without being roughly equally good. My response picks up on the idea that the "grading system" used to evaluate certain sets of options may have to employ broadly applicable evaluative terms. The result is broad evaluative classes (or leagues or neighborhoods) for which it is *not* safe to assume that all of the options that are in the same evaluative class are close enough in value to count as roughly equally good; indeed, for some pairs of options in the same class, it can be clear that one of the options is more than a little better than the other. Still, because, in accordance with the setup of the scenario provided, no more refined grading system is applicable, two options in the same evaluative class (or league or neighborhood) that are neither one better than the other nor exactly equally good are plausibly counted as on a par.

In Chapter 5, I turn to the question of whether incommensurable options can invariably be understood as being on a par or whether some incommensurable options are strictly incomparable. The small-improvement argument is sometimes put forward as an argument for incomparability. But, even if there are genuine small-improvement cases in which A is not better than B, B is not better than A, and yet A and B do not qualify as exactly equally good because A+, which is a slightly improved version of A, is better than A but not better than B, such cases can be cases of parity. Moreover, options that are on a par are comparable as "in the same league" and so are not completely incomparable (in terms of their overall value—i.e., in terms of how valuable they are overall—relative to what matters, from the point of view of practical reason, in the case at hand). Indeed, since the small-improvement argument invariably involves an only slightly improved version of one of the options, any real instance of the argument seems to support the possibility of parity rather than of incomparability.

In light of this challenge to the small-improvement argument as an argument for incomparability, I propose and consider the viability of a related, seemingly more promising argument that I call *the huge-improvement argument for incomparability*. Ultimately, there seems to be a way around this argument too, but reflection on the argument and on getting around it is revealing. It suggests that if there are any cases of incomparability, the really interesting phenomenon in such cases is not *between* the options but *within* the options, or at least within one of them: more specifically, it suggests that cases of incomparability, if there are any, are cases in which at least one of the options is resistant to classification as positive, negative, or fairly neutral. The answer to the question of whether every (contextualized) option can be classified as positive, negative, or fairly neutral is not obvious. I put forward a candidate case of an option that cannot be so classified, and a supporting argument, namely *the huge-improvement argument for resistance to overall evaluative classification*. This argument seems to provide a promising basis for the possibility of incomparability, but consideration of an important complication suggests that there remains a gap between the possibility of options that are resistant to classification as positive, negative, or fairly neutral, and the possibility of incomparability. In the end, what matters is that we recognize that, whether or not options can be strictly incomparable, there is room for cases beyond not just classic cases of *trichotomous comparability* (in which the options can be compared as either one better than the other or else as exactly equally good) but even beyond cases involving options that, although not trichotomously comparable, are still comparable as both positive, or both negative, or both fairly neutral. In the relevant further cases, at least one option is not positive, negative, neutral, or even fairly neutral. To the extent that comparability is revealed as applicable in such cases, skepticism about incomparability can persist, but its significance is reduced by the revelation of how little comparability requires.

In Chapter 6, I delve into the question of how the "better than" relation is best understood if rational preferences can be as disorderly as I have been suggesting. I focus especially on the following question: If rational preferences can be cyclic, what should we conclude about the presumed acyclicity of the "better than" relation? I argue that, in the name of preserving a construal of "better than" that fits with the idea that respecting betterness judgments is crucial to making good choices, we should stick with the idea that "better than" is acyclic and reject the assumption that "X is rationally preferred to Y (by A)" implies "X is better than Y (as an option for A)." As I explain, we can do this by accepting the *inadvisability condition*—according to which "X is better than Y (as an option for A)" implies that it is rationally inadvisable (for A) to choose Y from any finite set (of alternatives) that includes both X and Y—and the *practicability assumption*—according to which rationality cannot be such that, even without having made any prior errors, one can be in a predicament wherein every option is rationally inadvisable.

Along the way, I emphasize that, although we can hang on to the acyclicity of the "better than" relation, given the possibility of rationally cyclic preferences, thinking in terms of appraisal categories or leagues continues to be crucial, since rational choice will still sometimes involve *league-based satisficing* relative to one's preferences, wherein one chooses an option that is in the highest available league but is dispreferred relative to some other available option. Interestingly, the importance of thinking in terms of leagues persists even if one refuses to recognize the possibility of rationally cyclic preferences and maintains instead that (1) seemingly rational preference cycles are purely illusory and that (2) although, in some hard cases, it is admittedly unrealistic, or perhaps even impossible to identify an option that is optimal relative to the agent's concerns, there is invariably some such option. Although this response presupposes, rather than supporting, the acyclicity of rational preferences, practically speaking, even if it were compelling, the need for league-based satisficing remains, since our ignorance would leave us with the same practical challenge as in cases involving genuine rational preference cycles.

In Chapter 7, I explore the proper role of resolutions and regret in cases where disorderly preferences breed temptation and threaten to lead to self-defeating patterns of choice. It is now commonly recognized that, in cases involving disorderly preferences, an agent can qualify as giving in to temptation even while acting in *accordance* with her current evaluative rankings. Intrigued by this possibility, some philosophers have taken up the task of accounting for the rational failure in play in such cases. Two (potentially compatible) lines of thought have been developed: according to one line of thought, the failure at issue comes down, more or less, to deviating from a well-grounded resolution; according to the other line of thought, the failure comes down, more or less, to deviating from a prior intention without being sufficiently responsive to the prospect of future regret in which one ends up wishing one had stuck to one's prior intention. Yet, the current appeals to resolutions and regret and some of the verdicts provided face some serious challenges. Building on recent work concerning instrumental rationality, and delving into some important complications concerning human psychology, I revisit the relevant cases of temptation and analyze them in a way that puts resolutions, rational failure, and regret in their proper places. According to the position I defend, the relevant instances of giving in to temptation, *considered individually,* are not, other things equal, instances of irrationality, and the rational permissibility of giving in is not affected, except incidentally, by the agent's having formed a prior intention on the matter. Relatedly, the object of warranted dissatisfaction in situations of the relevant type is generally not a single choice but rather a pattern of choices or omissions.

In Chapter 8, I move on from familiar cases of regret involving dissatisfaction with a prior choice and consider the possibility of regret in cases where the agent chooses with care, continues to endorse his prior choices as rational, but still mourns the loss of a foregone good. Intuitively, it might seem like, in continued endorsement cases, an agent's regret (if it is to make sense) must be tied to the idea that the forgone good is no better than the achieved good but is also not fully made up for by the achieved good because the goods are (too) different in kind. But, if the possibility of rationally cyclic preferences is taken seriously, it becomes clear that even in continued endorsement cases, mourning the loss of a forgone good need not be tied to the idea that the loss of the good is not fully made up for by the gain of a preferred or incomparable good of a different kind. Instead, it can be tied to the need to settle, via league-based satisficing, on a dispreferred alternative. Where such settling is required, regret on the part of the agent is appropriately grounded in the idea that, although his choice was defensible relative to his concerns, he deprived himself of a preferred alternative. In such a case, the agent's loss of the forgone good cannot be softened by the thought that the loss was necessary for the gain of a preferred or incomparable good.

In the conclusion of the book, I emphasize some key take-home messages, including the following: Although cyclic and incomplete preferences can pose challenges for effective choice over time, such preferences can be rationally permissible. What rationality requires is not that our preferences be neatly ordered but that we proceed with caution and with a willingness to show restraint so as to avoid realizing a self-defeating pattern of choice when our preferences are disorderly. Properly understanding the major pitfall associated with disorderly preferences and seeing how it can be averted involves recognizing that the subjective appraisal responses to which instrumental rationality is accountable go beyond the relational appraisal responses captured by an agent's preferences; they also include categorial subjective appraisal responses. The distinction between relational appraisal responses and categorial appraisal responses also illuminates the possibility and nature of parity, and it is closely related to a serious challenge to seemingly promising arguments in favor of the possibility of incomparability. The revisionary way of understanding instrumental rationality that is suggested by the distinction between categorial and relational appraisal responses includes an important place for league-based satisficing relative to disorderly preferences. It is also, however, compatible with the acyclicity of the "better than" relation. Significantly, while failing to engage in league-based satisficing and giving in to temptation can lead to a certain sort of regret, successfully evading temptation via league-based satisficing can lead to another sort of regret. In the end, the central take-home message of the book is that rationality can handle quite a lot of messiness; this is important, since rationality wouldn't be all that helpful if, whenever messiness threatened, we had to rush to its rescue rather than look to it for guidance.

1

Disorderly Preferences

Standard rational choice theory requires that agents' preferences be acyclic and complete. The requirements of acyclicity and completeness are associated with the idea that, if an agent's preferences satisfy a certain set of constraints that include acyclicity and completeness, maximization with respect to her preferences is a genuine possibility. But should we think that an agent with cyclic preferences or with incomplete preferences is necessarily irrational? As indicated in the introduction, my view is that the answer is "no." In this chapter, I first focus on choice situations in which cyclic preferences seem natural and consider why they might be seen as too disorderly to be rationally permissible. I then discuss how cyclic preference can be defended and how the most influential challenge to cyclic preferences, namely the money-pump argument, can be reinterpreted. I then turn to incomplete preferences, which raise similar concerns and can be defended in a similar way. Note that, throughout, "rational" will figure as shorthand for "instrumentally rational" or "not excluded by instrumental rationality." Note also that, as suggested in the introduction, preferences are here understood as relational subjective appraisal responses, and, relatedly, as attitudes that can sometimes but not always explain choice (which is also impacted by habits, plans, and subjective appraisal responses beyond the agent's preferences).[1]

---

[1] This way of understanding preferences is fairly standard. See Hansson and Grüne-Yanoff (2018) for some relevant discussion regarding the notion of preference.

Choosing Well. Chrisoula Andreou, Oxford University Press. © Oxford University Press 2023.
DOI: 10.1093/oso/9780197584132.003.0002

1.1 Cyclic Preferences, the Money-Pump Argument, and the Puzzle of the Self-Torturer

Choice situations often include multiple dimensions of concern. For instance, when choosing between laptops, an agent might be concerned with reliability and price. And, even when choosing between laptops of the same reliability and price, an agent might be concerned with both the size of the screen and the weight of the laptop. Now consider, in light of this fact, the following scenario: Suppose J can purchase one of three equally reliable, identically priced laptops: laptop A has a large screen but weighs four pounds; laptop B has a medium-sized screen and weighs three pounds; laptop C has a small screen but weighs two pounds. Given this situation, one can imagine J having the following preferences: He prefers laptop A over laptop B because the one-pound difference in weight is not significant enough to make J want to pass up on the larger screen size. Similarly, he prefers laptop B over laptop C. And yet, he prefers laptop C over laptop A because the two-pound difference in weight does make J want to pass up on the larger screen size.

Given the famous money-pump argument, developed by Donald Davidson, J. McKinsey, and Patrick Suppes (1955), it might seem clear that, whether or not J's preferences are natural, the fact that they are cyclic makes them irrational. Like Dutch book arguments regarding betting, in which the rationality of an agent is put into question because the agent is susceptible to having a book made against her (i.e., to accepting a series of bets which are such that she is bound to lose more than she will gain),[2] the money-pump argument is concerned with agents who are vulnerable to making a combination of choices that lead to a sure loss. According to the money-pump argument (as it is commonly construed and tangential qualifications aside), cyclic preferences are irrational because

---

[2] For a relatively recent survey article on Dutch book arguments, see Vineberg (2016).

they can prompt an agent to accept a series of trade offers that leaves her with the same option she began with, but with less money. Return to J's case. As in the original case, suppose J has the following cyclic preferences: he prefers laptop A to laptop B, laptop B to laptop C, and laptop C to laptop A. Suppose also, however, that J receives a gift of laptop C and a hundred dollars in spending money. Suppose finally that, given his preferences between the different laptops, J prefers (1) laptop B and one less dollar of spending money over laptop C, (2) laptop A and one less dollar of spending money over laptop B, and (3) laptop C and one less dollar of spending money over laptop A. (Here a dollar is presumed to figure as a very small cost that J would prefer to pay over sticking to a dispreferred laptop option. If a dollar seems too steep, make it a penny—or even a tiyin, which is worth a small fraction of a penny—instead. What's needed for the argument is that the agent would prefer to pay some tiny amount over sticking to a dispreferred option.) Then a series of trade opportunities can spell trouble for J. In particular, given the opportunity to trade his current laptop (C) and a dollar for laptop B, J's preferences will prompt him to make the trade. Given the further opportunity to trade his current laptop (B) and a dollar for laptop A, J's preferences will prompt him to trade again. And given the opportunity to trade his current laptop (A) and a dollar for laptop C, J's preferences will prompt him to make a third trade. But this series of trades leaves J with the laptop he started off with and only ninety-seven dollars. And, if trading opportunities keep popping up, J's situation may continue to deteriorate. Even though he values his spending money, his preferences make him susceptible to being used as a "money pump."

But the money-pump argument—and variations on it that show that an agent with cyclic preferences is susceptible to being money pumped even if they anticipate that more trades will be coming[3]—need not be interpreted as supporting the view that

---

[3] See Wlodek Rabinowicz's modified money-pump argument (Rabinowicz 2000) and Tom Dougherty's "deluxe" money-pump argument (Dougherty 2014).

cyclic preferences are irrational. What the money-pump argument suggests is that *either* cyclic preferences are irrational *or* a rational agent is not invariably guided by their preferences. As such, someone who thinks there is good reason to accept that cyclic preferences can be rational can interpret the money-pump argument as supporting the second disjunct, and so as undermining the assumption that a rational agent will invariably act on their preferences. (This raises the interesting question of what appraisals, apart from an agent's preferences, instrumental rationality could be accountable to, which will be addressed in Chapter 3.)

But is there reason to accept that cyclic preferences can be rational? Is there, in particular, any solid counterexample to the standard view that they cannot be rational? Consider, as a candidate counterexample, Warren Quinn's puzzle of the self-torturer (1993a), adjusted ever so slightly with an italicized qualification: Someone referred to as the self-torturer has an electric device with 1,001 settings (0, 1, 2, 3, ..., 1,000) attached to him. Raising the setting of the device increases the amount of electric current running through the self-torturer's body. The increments in current are so tiny that the self-torturer cannot tell the difference between adjacent settings—*or at least he cannot, with any confidence, determine whether he has moved up a setting just by the way he feels*[4]; and yet, he can easily distinguish settings that are far enough apart. Indeed, there are settings that would take the self-torturer to a state of excruciating pain. The self-torturer is provided with the following offer. Once a week he can compare all the different settings and then, if he so chooses, he can advance one setting. Advancing a setting gets him $10,000, but once he advances a setting he can never

---

[4] Quinn himself does not add the qualification "or at least he cannot, with any confidence, determine whether he has moved up a setting just by the way he feels," but I think the qualification helpfully averts some distracting complications. For, as Tenenbaum and Raffman emphasize, "the puzzle doesn't require adjacent settings of the dial to be indiscriminable. It seems equally rational to prefer large sums of money over nearly imperceptible, or even just slight, differences in pain and yet to prefer abject poverty over sustained agony; ... these seem to be the preferences of most ordinary agents" (2012, 94).

permanently return to a lower setting. The self-torturer would like to increase his fortune, but he also cares about how he feels. Given his concerns (and assuming they are not distorted by artificial sharpening), he finds himself with the following preferences: For any two settings n and $n+1$, the self-torturer prefers (all things considered) stopping at $n+1$ to stopping at n. This is perfectly understandable, since any difference in comfort between adjacent settings is so slight that the self-torturer cannot, with any confidence, determine whether he has moved up a setting just by the way he feels, but he gets \$10,000 at each advance. And yet, understandably, the self-torturer also prefers stopping at setting zero, where he feels fine, over stopping at setting 1,000, where he feels excruciating pain. The self-torturer's preferences are clearly cyclic, and yet, it seems dogmatic to dismiss them as irrational.

As we have seen, appealing to the money-pump argument does not vindicate the dismissal, since the argument supports a weaker conclusion than is normally drawn. In particular, one can accept that cyclic preferences can lead to self-defeating choices, but conclude, not that cyclic preferences are irrational, but that rationality requires agents to keep track of how their choices "add up" and to choose in a way that avoids options that are clearly unacceptable even if this involves choosing somewhat arbitrarily because there is no optimal option (relative to the agent's preferences).[5] It might be suggested that the lack of any optimal option is what makes cyclic preferences irrational.[6] But this is to assume (rather than argue) that cyclic preferences are irrational, and the same holds for the similar suggestion that, if a set of preferences is rational, there must be an optimal option, even if it is difficult to identify.[7]

---

[5] This possibility is neglected by the suggestion that an agent like the self-torturer has "a good reason to regard [his preferences] as mistaken, since . . . [he] will end up badly by adhering to [them]" (Voorhoeve and Binmore 2006, 110).

[6] See Gustafsson (2013). I will return to Gustafsson's position in Chapter 3, Section 3.5.

[7] This suggestion is closely related to the idea that, though "apparently reasonable," we should seek to find the mistakes someone with cyclic preferences like those of the self-torturer "might" be making and default to the assumption that the agent is making one

The idea that, if a set of preferences is rational, there must always be an optimal option is tied to the assumption that rational preferences can be represented as the result of maximizing relative to fixed weights assigned to each dimension of interest. But this assumption is challenged by the case of the self-torturer. And although the case is controversial in certain respects, it exemplifies a possibility that Larry Temkin clearly articulates, namely that "*together* a sufficient number of differences in degree can sometimes amount to a difference in kind"; and "the relative significance of factors relevant for comparing alternatives merely differing in degree, may differ from the relative significance of those factors for comparing alternatives differing in kind" (1996, 194). For instance, monetary payoff may be a very significant factor in a relational appraisal of certain aches or pains (given the agent's concerns) if the aches or pains differ merely in degree (e.g., one mildly uncomfortable state with a barely noticeably different mildly uncomfortable state); by contrast, monetary payoff may be an insignificant factor in a relational appraisal of certain aches or pains (given the agent's concerns) if the pains differ in kind (e.g., a mildly uncomfortable state versus an excruciatingly painful state). Without an argument suggesting that this sort of variation (in the relative significance of certain factors depending on what options are being compared) is not possible, and with the alternative interpretation of the money-pump argument provided above, according to which a rational agent is not invariably guided by her preferences, the assumption that cyclic preferences are irrational seems unwarranted. As Quinn maintains, theorists need to be wary of making things "too easy on [themselves]" and "too hard on the self-torturer" (1993a, 199),

or more of these mistakes—an idea that seems to be at play in Arntzenius and McCarthy (1997, section 4).

whose concerns, to quote Sergio Tenenbaum and Diana Raffman, seem "rationally innocent" (2012, 99).[8]

It is worth emphasizing that, while the case of the self-torturer is quite odd in certain respects,

> the self-torturer is not alone in his predicament. Most of us are like him in one way or another. We like to eat but also care about our appearance. Just one more bite will give us pleasure and won't make us look fatter; but very many bites will. (Quinn 1993a, 199)

So, even though Quinn's case of the self-torturer is wholly fictitious and even fantastical, no appeal to fiction is needed to support the suggestion that changes can accumulate in a way that speaks against naively following even perfectly rational preferences.

Notably, similar predicaments can occur at the level of collectives. In particular, where individually trivial effects are involved, as in the case of "creeping environmental problems" such as pollution,[9] an agent with perfectly understandable but cyclic preferences, whether it be an individual or a *unified* collective, can be drawn into taking a series of individual steps that together figure as a course of destruction. Notice, for example, that if a unified collective values a healthy community, but also values luxuries whose production or use promotes a carcinogenic environment, it can find itself in a situation that is structurally similar to the situation of the self-torturer. Like the self-torturer, such a collective must cope with the fact that while one more day, and perhaps even one more month of indulgence can provide great rewards without bringing about any

---

[8] Tenenbaum's and Raffman's defense of the self-torturer appeals to the idea of vague projects. Some discussion of their position is included in Chapter 7. An updated version of Tenenbaum's defense can be found in Tenenbaum (2020).

[9] The phrase "creeping environmental problems" is borrowed from Glantz (1999).

non-trivial alterations in (physical or psychic) health, sustained indulgence is far from innocuous.[10]

1.2 Incomplete Preferences, Incommensurable Alternatives, and the Small-Improvement Argument

Like cyclic preferences, incomplete preferences—wherein certain pairs of options are not ranked in relation to one another by the agent's preferences, not even as equally favored—are not accommodated by rational choice theory, which includes the requirement of completeness, according to which for all options X and Y, either X is preferred to Y, or Y is preferred to X, or one is indifferent between X and Y. And yet, as with cyclic preferences, incomplete preferences sometimes arise quite naturally. This is because certain very different options seem incommensurable in that neither option seems better than the other and yet the options do not seem exactly equally good either (relative to what matters in the case at hand).[11] If there are genuine cases of incommensurability, preference gaps seem not only perfectly natural but also perfectly appropriate. (Note that I here leave room for, without committing to, the view that what matters in a particular case is invariably relative to a single "covering value" that may have "multiple contributory values" (Chang 1997). When I use phrases such as "better overall," "better all things considered," or sometimes just "better" for short, they should be interpreted as "better relative to what matters in the case at hand," and as not prejudging the question of

---

[10] For some contributions to the debate regarding individually trivial effects and collective action problems, see, for example, Glover (1975), Parfit (1984), Temkin (2005), Kagan (2011), Nefsky (2012), and Budolfson (2018).

[11] As emphasized in Chang (1997), the term "incommensurability" is used in several different ways in the literature. I here adopt the usage that suits my purposes and leave it to the reader to substitute a different term if they prefer to save the term "incommensurability" for another notion.

whether what matters in a particular case is invariably relative to a single "covering value.")

Cases of incommensurability are supposed to be distinguishable from cases of equal goodness as follows: In cases of incommensurability, the options are such that, not only is neither option better than the other (at least not determinately so), but a slightly improved version of one of the options need not be better than the other option.[12] Suppose, to adapt a case put forward by Joseph Raz, that K is trying to decide between career package C, in which she is a clarinetist, and career package L, in which she is a lawyer. After taking into account financial considerations, fit with her interests and capabilities, lifestyle, reward structure, hours, and so on, she might, it seems, reasonably conclude that (1) C is not better than L and (2) L is not better than C. Now consider career package C+, where the terms of C+ are identical to the terms of C except for a slight increase in pay. It seems like K could, even after affirming that C+ is better than C, still plausibly think that C+ is not better than L. But, if C+ is better than C but not better than L, then C and L cannot, it seems, be equally good. We thus seem to have a case in which for two objects of choice X and Y, X is not better than Y, Y is not better than X, and X and Y are not equally good. This example figures as an instance of what is commonly referred to as *the small-improvement argument* for incommensurability. Such instances provide candidates for three options A, A+, and B such that

P1: A is not better than B
P2: B is not better than A
P3: A+ is better than A
P4: A+ is not better than B

Given the plausible assumption that if two options are exactly equally good, then a further option that is better than one of the

[12] See Broome (2001, 115, 119), Broome (2000, 23–25), and Raz (1986, 325–326).

options will be better than the other option as well, it follows that, in addition to not being one better than the other, A and B are not exactly equally good either.[13] (Recall that, as indicated above, the preceding assumption is not impacted by my reasoning about rationally cyclic preferences if, as I argue in Chapter 6, "better than" can and should be understood as acyclic even if "is rationally preferred to" is not.)[14]

But there are some complications to consider. For instance, unless K is absurdly confident, she will presumably recognize her comparison of the career packages as extremely limited given all the factors that might be relevant to assessing them. Even if we assume that what K cares about determines what matters in the choice at hand, the assessment task can remain extremely difficult. For example, caring about, among other things, how satisfied she will feel, K may have to make some judgments about how certain features of the career packages are likely to affect her level of satisfaction—judgments that are likely to figure as, at best, decent estimates. While the difficulty of the assessment task makes it plausible that K cannot rank C as better than L, L as better than C, or C and L as equally good, it also suggests that this may be no indication that C and L are not commensurable, but only an indication of K's

---

[13] For a clear and concise discussion of the small-improvement argument (which, as will be discussed in Chapter 5, is also often cast as an argument for *incomparability*), see Chang (1997, section III.7). See also, and more recently, Chang (2017). Earlier variations on the argument can be found in, for example, Raz (1986, chapter 13), and de Sousa (1974). See, relatedly, Savage (1972, 17), wherein Savage considers a "test for indifference" according to which "if [a] person really does regard f and g as equivalent, that is, if he is indifferent between them, then, if f or g were modified by attaching an arbitrarily small bonus to its consequences in every state, the person's decision would presumably be for whichever act was thus modified."

[14] Note also that, although Johan Gustafsson and Nicolas Espinoza (2010) raise a worry about an analogous assumption in an analogous small-improvement argument, the worry is addressed by Erik Carlson (2011a), who shows how a modification can get around the worry. I won't delve into the analogous argument, the worry raised, or the modification for getting around the worry, since that would take me on a lengthy tangent. Insofar as there is a corresponding worry for the small-improvement argument that I am concerned with, there is also a corresponding solution (at least if, as I suggest in Chapter 6, we can and should understand betterness in a way that avoids the conclusion that being led by correct betterness judgments can be self-defeating).

epistemic limitations.[15] Given that comparing the options is an extremely difficult task (except, we are supposing, for the comparison
between C and C+, which is easily settled in favor of C+), it may be
that K's judgments "C is not better than L," "L is not better than C,"
and "C+ is not better than L" are more accurately understood as "I
cannot safely conclude, on the basis of the available evidence, that
C is better than L," "I cannot safely conclude, on the basis of the
available evidence, that L is better than C," and "I cannot safely conclude, on the basis of the available evidence, that C+ is better than
L." But this latter set of judgments is consistent with C and L being
commensurable.

There are, however, some possible hard case scenarios that are not
properly interpreted as cases of ignorance. Suppose, for example,
that what matters in a particular situation is what is appealing relative to the agent's subjective, sensibility-issued valuations, and that,
as a matter of fact, the agent's sensibility is such that it simply does
not generate a comparative subjective valuation between options
that are experienced as "in the same league" but also appealing in
very different ways.[16] In such a case, the agent can, without error,
judge that, given what matters in the case at hand, A is not better
than B, B is not better than A, A+ is better than A, but A+ is not
better than B. Ruth Chang's coffee or tea case can be interpreted as a
case of the relevant sort:

> Suppose you must determine which of a cup of coffee and a cup of
> tea tastes better to you. The coffee has a full-bodied, sharp, pun-
> gent taste, and the tea has a warm, soothing, fragrant taste. It is
> surely possible that you rationally judge that the cup of Sumatra
> Gold tastes neither better nor worse than the cup of Pearl Jasmine
> and that although a slightly more fragrant Jasmine would taste

---

[15] Discussion of this complication can be found in, for example, Regan (1997).
[16] I say more about this possibility in "Preferences, Proxies, and Rationality"
(unpublished).

better than the original, the more fragrant Jasmine would not taste better than the cup of coffee. (2002a, 669)

Relatedly, if you are sampling the beverages for the purposes of choice, and correctly believe that, in the context at hand, one beverage is better than the other for the purposes of choice only if, given your sensibility, it tastes better to you, then you can, it seems, judge, without error, that the cup of Sumatra Gold is neither better nor worse than the cup of Pearl Jasmine, and that although a slightly more fragrant Jasmine would be better than the original,[17] the more fragrant Jasmine would not be better than the cup of coffee. Moreover, a preference gap between the original cup of Sumatra Gold and the original cup of Pearl Jasmine seems perfectly appropriate, as does a preference gap between the Sumatra Gold and the slightly more fragrant Jasmine. (More on this in Chapter 4.)

Still, like an agent with cyclic preferences, an agent with incomplete preferences is susceptible to self-defeating behavior. More specifically, the agent is susceptible to incurring a gratuitous cost after taking a series of steps each of which seems permissible. Consider, for example, an agent, P, whose preferences are incomplete (due, let us suppose, to incommensurability), with neither X and Y ranked in relation to one another, nor X+ and Y ranked in relation to one another. Having no preference between X+ and Y, P might, at R's suggestion, be willing to trade X+ for Y. Moreover, having no preference between Y and X, she might then, at T's suggestion, be willing to trade Y for X. This series of choices, which takes P from X+ to X, seems regrettable.

But, as with the money-pump argument in the case of cyclic preferences, we need not interpret this potential pitfall as showing that the agent's preferences are problematic. Instead, there is room

---

[17] Note that the betterness of a slightly more fragrant Jasmine in this case fits neatly with my discussion of alternatives with one disadvantageous difference in Chapter 3 and my discussion of the "inadvisability condition" in Chapter 6.

for the view that incomplete preferences are permissible, and the pitfall under consideration can be avoided so long as the agent proceeds with care. The agent might, for example, take care to avoid "brute shuffling," where (roughly put) such shuffling involves settling on an option and then switching to another without a decisive reason to do so.[18] Notably, the question of whether there is a rational prohibition against brute shuffling even if it does not result in a gratuitous cost is controversial. For reasons that will emerge in the next chapter, I myself think that brute shuffling can be permissible, so long as the agent avoids self-defeating behavior by, for example, tracking things like whether a particular instance of brute shuffling would qualify as a shuffle to a worse version of an option she shuffled away from before.[19]

---

[18] See Bratman (2012) for some influential discussion regarding the possibility of a rational prohibition against "brute shuffling." For interesting, related discussion, see, for example, Ferrero (2012).

[19] See, relatedly, Andreou (2005).

2

Self-Defeating Self-Governance

As is clear from Chapter 1, agents with cyclic and incomplete preferences must carefully guard against self-defeating behavior. This chapter identifies the nature of the self-defeating behavior at issue as a form of *self-defeating self-governance*. According to one familiar way of understanding self-defeating behavior, cases of self-defeating behavior, if they are not the result of misinformation, are due to the self failing to govern behavior. This occurs if, for example, the values that the agent identifies with are defeated by some desire that the agent is subject to but does not identify with. There is, however, a stricter sense of self-defeating behavior according to which the self that is defeated and the self doing the defeating are one and the same; in particular, the values that the self identifies with are defeated even though nothing "alien" is guiding the self. The possibility of informed self-defeating self-governance is puzzling if one abstracts away from cyclic and incomplete preferences. This chapter reveals the connections between cyclic preferences, incomplete preferences, and informed self-defeating self-governance. In short, the self-defeating patterns of choice that agents with cyclic and incomplete preferences must guard against are not to be explained in terms of the self losing control over behavior but as instances of informed self-defeating self-governance.

2.1 Self-Governance

You are sitting in the back seat of the car minding your own business when your older brother picks up your hand and uses it to slap

Choosing Well. Chrisoula Andreou, Oxford University Press. © Oxford University Press 2023.
DOI: 10.1093/oso/9780197584132.003.0003

you in the face repeatedly, chanting all the while "Why are you hit-ting yourself?" The question must of course be rejected. You are not hitting yourself; rather, your brother is hitting you with your hand. As is plain to see, it is he that is controlling your movement, not you. In other cases, such as when one is behaving in accordance with instructions provided at an earlier time while one was under hypnosis, it is less transparent, at least to oneself, that one is being controlled by someone else; and, indeed, the expectation that one is controlling one's own behavior may lead to creative confabulations concerning why it is that one is doing what one finds oneself doing.[1] Still, the illusion of self-governance in such cases is just that—an illusion. One is not self-governed if one is being controlled by someone else.

The two sorts of cases considered so far can naturally be described as cases in which one figures as a puppet with someone else pulling the strings. But, as the idea of self-governance has been understood, one can lack self-governance even if one is not being controlled by some outside agent. For, according to the philosophically rich no-tion of self-governance that I am interested in, one does not count as self-governed if (or to the extent that) one is governed by some-thing with which one does not identify or which one finds alien, and this includes desires that one could honestly disown, even if they have not been implanted by another. A classic case of the rele-vant sort is the case of the unwilling addict, who finds herself with a desire for a drug but does not identify with this desire, and in-deed sees fighting the desire as essential to expressing her "true" self (where her "true" self need not be some homuncular entity, but can be a theoretical construct defined, roughly speaking, by the agent's commitments and values).[2] The true self associated with the rich

---

[1] See Wegner (2002), particularly chapter 5, for some intriguing experimental work concerning such confabulations.

[2] This case has been prominent in debates on self-governance, particularly since Harry Frankfurt's influential paper "Freedom of the Will and the Concept of a Person" (1971).

notion of self-governance under consideration is the controlling self implicit in the idea of self-control. Someone does not count as exhibiting self-control just because they act on their desires; to the contrary, if the desires they act on are ones they disown, they count as lacking self-control. (This is not to say that their behavior should be excused, although we do often find "crimes of passion" being treated more leniently than crimes in which the perpetrator is not "carried away" by a desire.)

Different views of self-governance flesh out this skeletal description in different ways, but one point that seems to figure as common ground is that if one is self-governed, one is governed by one's commitments and values.[3] Being governed by one's commitments and values is just a necessary condition of self-governance, not a sufficient one, and it is no easy philosophical matter to provide a theory of valuing. But the aim of this section is just to focus our attention on the notion of self-governance that I am interested in, not to delve into current theories of valuing.

For the purposes of this discussion (apart from Section 2.5, wherein a qualification that we can put aside for the moment will be introduced), if A's values or commitments change between time 1 and time 2, then A1 (A at time 1) will not count as the same self as A2 (A at time 2), even though A1 and A2 may, for the purposes of personal identity, count as the same person. This allows us to say that if one is constrained to act in accordance with values and commitments one no longer has, this is no more a case of self-governance than if one is constrained to act in accordance with the alien values and commitments of another person. In short, self-governed behavior is governed by currently held values and

---

[3] See Bratman (2007) for a sense of the history and recent state of the debate on self-governance. Bratman (2003) focuses on the "Platonic challenge" to the "Frankfurtian" approach. See, relatedly, Frankfurt (1971) and Watson (1975, 1987).

commitments (which may, we can allow, reflect a collective or di-achronic perspective prompted by identification with a larger whole).

2.2 Self-Defeating Behavior

Like self-governed behavior, self-defeating behavior—at least in the strict sense that concerns me here and that is, in my view, crucial to discussions of diachronic rationality, which are specifically concerned with choice over time rather than with choice at a time—must be such that it can be traced to the self, rather than to something alien to the self. Relatedly, in self-defeating behavior, the one being defeated is the same as the one doing the defeating. You can be defeated by a barrage of face-slaps, but this is not a case of self-defeat if your brother is the one hitting you, even if it is with your own hand. One can be defeated by a steady intake of drugs, but if one's drug taking cannot be traced to one's (true) self (but is instead the product of alien, disowned desires), then again this is not a case of self-defeat. Since self-defeating behavior (strictly understood) must be such that it can be traced to the self, self-defeating behavior must be self-governed.

It is easy to engage in self-governed, self-defeating behavior if one is misled by false beliefs about the consequences of some of the choices one is making. Suppose, for example, that one values being liked by one's co-workers and believes that ridiculing one's boss will make one quite popular; but, in fact, such behavior will have the opposite effect. Then, when one ridicules one's boss, one is, other things equal, engaging in self-governed, self-defeating behavior. Similarly, self-governed, self-defeating behavior can easily result when the consequences of some of one's choices are uncertain. If, to borrow an example from John Brunero, an investor makes a risky but reasonable investment with the aim of getting out of debt, but the project in which he invests is a failure and he actually ends up further into debt, his behavior may well be both self-governed and self-defeating.[4]

But, putting aside such cases involving faulty beliefs or uncertainty about the consequences of one's choices, it seems like self-governed behavior cannot be self-defeating. For, consider the following line of reasoning:

> If one's behavior is self-governed, it is governed by values and commitments with which one identifies and which one does not find alien; and so, one's behavior is true to oneself. Assuming it is based on an awareness of the consequences of each choice one makes, behavior that is true to oneself does not also defeat this same self, and so self-governed behavior is not self-defeating.[5,6]

We are thus left with a dilemma that seems to undermine the possibility of informed self-defeating behavior. On the one hand, given that self-defeat involves being defeated by oneself, if some behavior is not self-governed, it cannot be self-defeating. On the

---

[4] Brunero, personal communication, July 2010.

[5] Since achieving something one values may require making sacrifices and, more specifically, incurring some harm, one's behavior can be self-destructive without being self-defeating.

[6] A few words about this line of reasoning in relation to the paradox of hedonism (an in-depth treatment of which is outside the scope of this book): If pursuing pleasure directly (where this is to be cashed out in part in terms of "mental" actions, such as directing one's attention in certain ways and monitoring certain responses) is not an effective means to attaining pleasure—as per the paradox of hedonism—then someone that pursues pleasure directly with the aim of attaining it is, it seems, being misled by a false belief (concerning the utility of certain mental actions) or else "carried away" by an impulse that she thinks she should resist (namely the impulse to pursue pleasure directly, which is distinct from and in some sense more abstract than impulses toward particular activities pursued for their own sake that bring one pleasure). So, such behavior is, it seems, either self-defeating but not well-informed, or not self-governed and so not self-defeating (even if the impulse to pursue pleasure directly is itself in some sense self-defeating). Thus, this is not a case (or at least not a clear case) of informed self-defeating behavior. More modestly, it is not a case that I am prepared to use to defend the possibility of informed self-defeating behavior.

other hand, given that self-governance involves being true to oneself, if some behavior is self-governed, it cannot, assuming it is informed, be self-defeating. So, it seems that, if informed, neither self-governed behavior nor behavior that is not self-governed can be self-defeating. (Note that, henceforth, the qualification "informed" will often be left implicit.)

One response to this dilemma is to grant that self-defeating behavior, understood as behavior involving the defeat of one's self by one's self—where the self in question is defined, roughly speaking, in terms of one's commitments and values—is indeed impossible, but to stress that in a looser sense, wherein self-defeat involves the defeat of one's self by desires and behaviors that one disowns despite recognizing them as in some sense own's own, self-defeating behavior is possible. In this weaker sense, the classic case of the unwilling addict, who persistently disowns her desire for drugs even as she persistently seeks out drugs, is a case of self-defeating behavior.

I can certainly see why one would be willing to loosen up the notion of self-defeat and count the classic case of the unwilling addict as a case of self-defeat, but here I want to focus on vindicating the possibility of behavior that is self-defeating in a stronger sense—a sense in which the desires and behaviors that are defeating one's self are ones with which one identifies. The possibility of self-defeat in this stronger sense is, I think, inextricably tied to the existence of certain diachronic rationality constraints. I will move away from the classic case of the unwilling addict and consider two other types of cases in which it is tempting to say that the agent's behavior is self-defeating. The first case, which involves preference reversals, gets us closer than the classic case of the unwilling addict to a case of strictly self-defeating behavior. The second case, which involves cyclic preferences, arguably gets us all the way there. After considering the second case, I turn to interesting complications raised by cases involving incommensurable alternatives.

2.3 The Satisfied Slice

The theoretical literature on addiction includes a great deal of interesting discussion relating addictive behavior to discounting-induced preference reversals.[7] Human beings discount future utility and do so in a way that can result in problematic preference reversals. Consider the following case: J must repeatedly decide whether to smoke a cigarette or not. Suppose he values the pleasures of smoking but also values his health; furthermore, his preference between smoking and not smoking with respect to a particular upcoming smoking opportunity is determined by his comparing the discounted values he assigns to the options under consideration. Now suppose that when contemplating each of n smoking opportunities in advance, he prefers to refrain in each of these cases rather than to indulge. But as each smoking opportunity becomes imminent, the discounted value he assigns to indulging in the case at hand can overtake the discounted value of refraining, particularly if his discount rate for imminent rewards is very low while his discount rate for non-imminent rewards is high. If it does, then his preference between smoking in this case and not smoking in this case will reverse; and if such discounting-induced preference reversals become the rule, he will repeatedly indulge rather than repeatedly refraining.

As in the classic case of the unwilling addict, it is tempting to say that J's behavior is self-defeating. But whereas in the classic case, the unwilling addict is being defeated by desires he disowns even while they are moving him, J's choice at each choice point can be construed as governed by a time slice of himself that is satisfied with its choice. By hypothesis, this time slice, like J's other time slices, has no principled objection against smoking. It simply takes the rewards and costs of smoking into account, discounts them according to their distance into the future, and chooses accordingly.

---

[7] See especially George Ainslie's work and, in particular, Ainslie (2001).

The time slice's decision, however, is unpopular with most of the other time slices anticipating the opportunity, because, given their different temporal locations and despite their shared weighing procedure, the other slices can and generally do have the opposite preference regarding the particular opportunity in question.

Because J's choice at each choice point can be construed as governed by a time slice of himself that is satisfied with its choice, J's choice seems more his own than the choice of the addict in the classic unwilling addict case. And yet, J's case still does not seem like a case of self-defeating behavior in the strongest sense, wherein the self that is doing the defeating is identical to the self that is being defeated. Instead, the case is one in which one time-slice self is defeating other time-slice selves (with conflicting preferences). And even if each time-slice self has a turn doing some defeating, the defeat of an aggregate('s members) by the aggregate('s members) need not count as self-defeat, as is evident if one considers the case in which A and B defeat A and B via A's destroying B's chances at happiness and B's destroying A's chances at happiness. As this last point suggests, J's case is very similar to the case of the waverer who switches back and forth between two incompatible goals. Both cases fit with the possibility of situations in which changing priorities fragment a person into conflicting and competing transitory selves.

2.4 Strictly Self-Defeating Behavior

I turn now to a structurally different sort of case that I think gets us strictly self-defeating behavior—a case involving cyclic preferences. K very much enjoys the pleasures of eating and has a wonderful caretaker who provides her with three lovely meals a day. K has little acquaintance with her fridge, although a few times when her caretaker has been sick K has had to venture to her fridge and forage for food herself. K's caretaker supplies her with a steady but well-paced supply of treats and so K happily enjoys both delicious desserts and decent health. She values both and feels no guilt whatsoever when she bites into a luscious brownie, or creamy pudding after dinner. Although she realizes that this is not the most nourishing thing she could be consuming and could easily request something else, she is perfectly happy to give up some nutritional value for a surge of gustatory pleasure. And, to date, her health has been good. But at some point, K is separated from her caretaker. Perhaps her caretaker dies, or K goes off to college. The main thing is that K begins to increase her interaction with her fridge. As usual, when faced with treats, she often willingly gives up some nutritional value for a surge of gustatory pleasure, perhaps occasionally noting that whether she ends her current meal with fresh fruit or fried ice cream is trivial in terms of affecting her health status, since the transition from decent health to poor health is not the product of a single culinary indulgence of this sort. Within a year or so, K has become very overweight and has gradually developed some associated health problems (such as, perhaps, joint pain). She has not done justice to her valuing of decent health and vows to find an intermediary between herself and her fridge and to get back on track.[8]

Unlike J's situation, K's situation does not assume that she is experiencing preference reversals. And it does not assume that K is experiencing increasingly heightened or irresistible cravings for treats that transform her values or subject her to desires that she disowns (or that she would have originally disowned). Although K's situation changes, her values and preferences can be perfectly constant. She values decent health and the pleasures of eating, and these are the values that are in play when, taking into account that

---

[8] It might be tempting to assume that K's behavior reveals that she doesn't—or at least didn't—really value good health; but, given the possibility of cyclic preferences, we can make sense of an agent's being drawn into taking a series of individual steps to an outcome that she avows is much worse than other outcomes that were available without assuming that the agent must be hypocritical or deceived about what she really cares about. For related discussion, see, for example, Andreou (2007b).

her current choice will not significantly affect her health status, she gives up some nutritional value for a surge of gustatory pleasure. (I here assume, as K does, that, at each choice point, K's opting for a treat does not rule out her showing restraint on future occasions.)[9] Of course, as pretty much everybody knows (including, by hypothesis, K), a series of individually trivial effects can accumulate in a way that gradually (i.e., without any sudden substantial fall off) results in non-trivial negative effects, and this is precisely what happens when K loses her caretaker. (Although it is not difficult to imagine a version of K's case in which K is led astray by false beliefs about the consequences of some of her choices, especially if K is quite young, it is also not difficult to imagine a case in which K's problem is not a lack of information about the consequences of each choice she is making in the context in which the choice is made. The latter sort of case is in play here.) Her individual choices after she loses her caretaker seem no less self-governed than before, indeed if anything they seem more self-governed, and yet they collectively constitute a self-defeating course of action. And here the self that is doing the defeating really does seem to be identical to the self that is being defeated. The self in question is K's temporally extended self—a self that is unified by, among other things, stable but cyclic preferences. Putting aside tangential complications, and allowing that K will have a fixed number of indulgence opportunities this

---

[9] Relatedly, I accept, as a background assumption, the standard view that, roughly put, the option of φ-ing at t' (or from t through t' if, as is normally the case, φ-ing takes time) is currently open to A (where A is a temporally extended agent that will persist until at least t') so long as (where this flags a sufficient condition) A would φ at t' (or from t through t') if she were to exert her control accordingly between now and t'. (Notably, someone too fleeting or susceptible to disintegration to endure as the same agent until t' would, by hypothesis, not endure long enough to (herself) carry out anything at t'—or from t through t'—including any resolution based on the faulty assumption that she will endure until t', and so the question of whether φ-ing at t'—or from t through t'—is open to her is invariably "no." There is no reason to assume K is fragmented in this way.) For some innovative and thought-provoking discussion regarding an agent's options, see Portmore (2019). Although addressing Portmore's discussion falls outside the scope of this book, I raise what I see as serious concerns about it in "Agency, Options, and Control" (unpublished).

Figure 2.1 Read "Y< X" as "X is preferred to Y."

year, say 1,000, we can assume that for any *n* less than 1,000, K prefers to indulge *n+1* times in all than to indulge *n* times in all, but she also prefers to indulge only occasionally (or even never) than to indulge so often that she becomes unhealthy. She therefore finds herself with the preference loop in **Figure 2.1**. When K bites into a brownie, it is not a time slice of herself that is governing against the opposing preferences and values of other time slices. All of K's time-slice selves share the preferences and values relevant to this opportunity for enjoyment.

Now it might be objected that although K's values are stable over time, they are inconsistent and so they cannot be the basis of self-governed behavior, which assumes a sufficiently coherent stance. Let me grant, at least for the moment and for the sake of argument, that there is something to the idea that self-governance (in a domain) is possible only if one's values are sufficiently coherent.[10] For

---

[10] This idea is related to a point made by Bratman (2009) that is briefly discussed in note 13 below.

instance, whether one sees Dr. Jekyll and Mr. Hyde as two distinct selves or as a single but dual self, one might insist that the package contains too many contradictory moral stances for self-governed moral behavior. Still, in relation to K's case, the charge of inconsistency just seems to point to the fact that K's values are such that they can, in certain situations, lead her to a self-defeating course of action; and this may warrant the claim that she is not optimally organized (although I'm not sure it does), but it does not seem to follow that her values cannot form the basis of self-governed behavior (or that she fails to count as a single self). Presumably self-governance does not depend on having all-purpose worked-out values and weighing systems that never lead one into any trouble no matter what comes up or how one's situation changes.[11] Herein lies the possibility of strictly self-defeating behavior (even for a creature who not only has wants, but also has values that build on her reflections about whether she wants these wants to figure as reasons in her practical deliberation).

Quite plausibly, if some of my self-governed behavior is self-defeating (despite each choice being made in light of accurate information about its consequences in the context in which it is made), I should do something about this. Perhaps I can resolve to make individual decisions in accordance with an overall plan with which I am satisfied given my existing values and my choice situation. Or perhaps I can undergo a process that will change some of my preferences, making resoluteness unnecessary. Moreover, it may be that once I do something of this sort, I have changed myself enough, disowning some of what I previously owned, to make any continuing self-defeating behavior self-defeating only in a weak

[11] Elijah Millgram's view on hyperspecialization (in Millgram 2009) suggests that serial hyperspecializers do well in rapidly changing environments because their values and weighing systems change as their situations do. Humans may be serial hyperspecializers, and it may be that perfect serial hyperspecializers would never engage in self-defeating behavior, but, as Millgram would presumably grant, we aren't *perfect* when it comes to adapting to rapid change.

sense, such as the sense in which the classic case of the unwilling addict involves self-defeating behavior. Even if this is so, it cannot be concluded that strictly self-defeating behavior is rare. And it is certainly not the case that resolutions or preference changes are *bound* to occur well in advance of any trouble whenever one's values are such that they can, given certain series of choice situations, lead one to a self-defeating course of action. As such, if my reasoning so far is correct, strictly self-defeating behavior, which can also be described as self-defeating self-governance, is, contrary to initial appearances, definitely possible.

2.5 A Complication

There is a complication that is particularly interesting with respect to the existence of diachronic rationality constraints that is glossed over in my discussion and to which I now want to return. At least part of the answer to the question "Are there any diachronic rationality constraints on agents?" is "Yes, agents must avoid self-defeating behavior." I now want to refine the notion of the self with which I started off, and then suggest that self-defeating behavior may encompass all cases of diachronic irrationality, in which case the answer that I have provided to the question of whether there are any diachronic rationality constraints on agents will be a complete rather than partial answer to the question posed.

So far, I have been relying on a notion of the self according to which the self is defined by values and commitments so that when one's values and commitments change, so does one's self. This notion of the self allows us to say that if one is constrained to act in accordance with values and commitments one no longer has, one is not self-governed. But we can refine this notion of the self in a way that is useful in thinking about diachronic rationality and self-defeating behavior while hanging on to the idea that self-governed behavior is governed by currently held values and commitments. In particular, we can refine the notion so that the self is understood in terms of values and commitments that have "taken root." (Note that if one is fragmented over time, a commitment that is firmly rooted now can fail to be long-lived.)

To see how the suggested refinement can be relevant, consider the following situation: Suppose one finds two ends incommensurable in that one cannot rank them in relation to one another; and yet one must choose between them. Let us focus on the case of Abraham as described by John Broome:

> God tells Abraham to take his son Isaac to the mountain, and there sacrifice him. Abraham has to decide whether or not to obey. Let us assume this is one of those choices where the alternatives are incommensurate. The option of obeying will show submission to God, but the option of disobeying will save Isaac's life. Submitting to God and saving the life of one's son are such different values that they cannot be weighed determinately against each other; that is the assumption. Neither option is better than the other, yet we also cannot say that they are equally good. (2001, 114)

Suppose Abraham commits to obeying God. He thus takes Isaac to the foot of the mountain. Once there, however, he wavers, commits to saving Isaac (which remains incommensurable with obeying God), and thus backtracks. Following Broome, let us assume that "turning back at the foot of the mountain is definitely worse than never having set out at all" since "trust between father and son [has already been] badly damaged" (115).[12] Is Abraham's self stable enough to make this course of behavior count as strictly self-defeating?

Note that I assume that Abraham's taking Isaac to the foot of the mountain is a self-governed action and that Abraham's turning back

---

[12] Recall that two alternatives, one of which is definitely worse than the other, can both be incommensurable with a third alternative.

is a self-governed action. More generally, I assume that if an action is governed by a value that is a central part of oneself (and no logically contradictory value also figures as a central part of oneself, i.e., there is no Jekyll-and-Hyde type duality in play), then the action is self-governed, even if one remains torn between the demands of the value one acts on and the currently competing demands of another value that is also a central part of oneself.[13] I also assume that Abraham's behavior counts as self-governed *over time* (in the sense that is required for strictly self-defeating behavior) *if* his behavior is governed by a self that is (sufficiently) stable over the relevant time frame.[14]

As the case is described by Broome, Abraham's wavering may well be due to the (stable) incommensurability between the options he faces rather than due to any changes in perspective on Abraham's part. Although, or perhaps because, Abraham deeply and consistently values both submitting to God and saving his son, it may be

---

[13] In "Intention, Practical Rationality, and Self-Governance" (2009), Bratman argues that while self-governance (at a time) is possible when, or in a domain where, one has conflicting desires, it is not possible in a domain where one (concurrently) has inconsistent intentions or has incoherent means-end plans; for, in a domain of the latter sort, there cannot be a clear answer to the question of where one stands and "it is only if there is a place where you stand that *you* are governing in the corresponding domain" (431). It is interesting to think about this idea in relation to the possibility of self-governance (at a time) in cases where an action is governed by a value that is a central part of oneself while one remains torn between the demands of that value and the currently competing demands of another value that is also a central part of oneself. It might be suggested that in forming an intention to act in accordance with one of the values, one is (even if only temporarily) taking a stand despite being torn, and that is what is crucial for the possibility of self-governance (at a time), (which is not to say this is enough for self-governance over time). But in my view, the possibility of self-governance (at a time) in this case is tied to one's acting on a deeply held value, not to one's (stand-taking) intention, which is arguably too superficial to qualify as among one's self-defining (or self-constituting) attitudes. See, relatedly, note 14.

[14] If Abraham's original intention to sacrifice Isaac and his later intention to save Isaac are each in turn seen as among Abraham's self-defining attitudes, then Abraham's wavering compromises his self-governance over time, since it compromises the existence of a stable self. But if these particular intentions are not included among Abraham's self-defining attitudes (while his valuing of God and Isaac are included), then although Abraham's wavering may be self-defeating and/or irrational, it need not imply a lack of self-governance over time. Abraham may just be failing to do a good job governing himself over time. As I will explain presently, I find the latter interpretation quite compelling.

difficult for the specific commitment to obey God in this case (or, alternatively, to disobey God in this case) to take root. There is thus a sense in which a specific commitment can form on the surface, while the agent remains torn within. (This need not always happen in cases of incommensurability; and it is perhaps often countered by a sort of endowment effect, which facilitates retroactively seeing the option one chose as more valuable, which in turn promotes one's valuing it more thereafter.[15]) When wavering reflects an agent's being torn all along, with no specific commitment really taking root, the agent's self-defeating behavior seems self-defeating in the strong sense according to which the self doing the defeating is the same as the self being defeated, namely the temporally extended self who deeply and stably values a variety of goods that are of very different sorts and that cannot always be combined or ranked in relation to one another.

If one can make a specific commitment without its taking root in oneself, then this makes more room for strictly self-defeating behavior. It also makes it quite easy to accept the idea that all cases of diachronic irrationality are cases of strictly self-defeating behavior, wherein the self doing the defeating is the same as the self being defeated. For, given any case of things going wrong over time, we can reason as follows: If, on the one hand, things are going wrong because the agent is deeply fragmented, fragmented enough that it does not make sense to think of the agent's actions as governed by a stable self, then, if we have a case of irrationality at all—and we need not—it will in essence be a case of collective irrationality, not a case of diachronic irrationality. If, on the other hand, things are going wrong even though the agent is not deeply fragmented but is instead governed by a stable self, then either (1) things are

---

[15] See Thaler (1980) for his influential discussion of the endowment effect with respect to consumer choices. In a nutshell, the effect of endowment at issue is that "people often demand much more to give up an object than they would be willing to pay to acquire it" (Kahneman, Knetsch, and Thaler 1991, 194), seemingly overvaluing what they currently have.

going wrong because the agent is violating an authoritative external standard, which may amount to irrationality but not diachronic irrationality, or (2) things are going wrong because the agent is defeating his own ends or values and is thus engaged in self-defeating behavior. This suggests that all cases of diachronic irrationality are cases of self-defeating behavior.

Importantly, to say that agents must avoid self-defeating behavior is not to say that preference structures that leave room for self-defeating behavior are irrational. For example, one can allow, as I do, that incomplete preferences, which reflect the stance that some alternatives are incommensurable, are rationally permissible while maintaining that allowing oneself to follow a self-defeating course of action on the basis of such preferences is irrational.[16]

Note also that I am not committed to the idea that switching plans from one that enjoins pursuing alternative A to one that enjoins pursuing an incommensurable alternative, A*, is invariably self-defeating and diachronically irrational. Suppose, for example, that although M, an engineering student, sees doing philosophy in their spare time and writing poetry in their spare time as incommensurable, they decide to spend the summer doing philosophy. Midsummer, after a month of rewarding philosophical reflection, they switch intentions and decide to dedicate their time and energy to writing poetry instead. It's *not*, let us suppose, that they have tired of philosophy or have come to think that they really must do a bit of both philosophy and poetry and so sticking with their initial intention is no longer rational. They simply allow themselves to follow what they sees as an incommensurable path. Here it seems that their switch in intentions, although not required, need not be self-defeating, in which case it need not, in my view, be diachronically irrational.[17]

---

[16] See Section 1.2 above, as well as Andreou (2005).

[17] Bratman (2012), restricting his attention to agents that are concerned with self-governance and assuming that such a concern grounds a normative reason in favor of self-governance, defends a stricter constraint concerning the permissibility of switching from one alternative to another in cases where the agent initially judged the alternatives

2.6 Conclusion

Paradigmatically, self-governed behavior is behavior that is true to oneself, while self-defeating behavior is behavior that is not true to oneself. This makes self-governed behavior and self-defeating behavior seem like opposites. But self-defeating behavior is self-defeating in the strict sense of interest in this chapter only if the self doing the defeating is identical to the self being defeated, where the self in question is defined, roughly speaking, in terms of the agent's commitments and values. This suggests that (strictly) self-defeating behavior must be self-governed. Reflecting on complications associated with how choices accumulate over time allows us to see how self-defeating behavior, understood as self-governed, is possible. The challenges of choice over time, even when one is not changing (in any deep way) over time, leave room for behavior that is faulty with respect to being true to oneself without involving false beliefs or uncertainty about the consequences of each choice one makes or a failure of self-governance. It follows that governance over time by a stable self is not sufficient for the avoidance of informed

incommensurable and the agent's evaluation of the alternatives has stayed the same. According to Bratman's proposed diachronic rationality constraint, which incorporates a default presumption in favor of prior intentions, switches of the relevant sort are fine in the context of a plan that calls for sampling different alternatives over time (pursuing each for just a while), since the switch does not actually violate one's earlier (qualified) intention to pursue the first alternative, but problematic when they involve genuinely abandoning an earlier intention (that is not qualified by a relevant "sampling plan"). Bratman labels cases of the latter sort (in the context described) cases of "brute shuffling" and characterizes brute shuffling as "locally irrational" (for agents concerned with self-governance and assuming that such a concern grounds a normative reason in favor of self-governance). I am not sure that Bratman and I disagree about brute shuffling, since Bratman might effectively argue that, relative to the agents he is concerned with and relative to his starting assumption concerning normativity and self-governance, brute shuffling is invariably self-defeating. In any case, my understanding is that we at least agree that it is appropriate to allow one's verdict on the rationality or irrationality of brute shuffling to fall out of one's more general views concerning diachronic rationality [personal communication]. Since this is not the place for me to delve further into Bratman's approach to understanding diachronic rationality (which includes developments and refinements that can be found in Bratman 2018), let me just say that I am here exploring a different (perhaps complementary) approach.

self-defeating behavior. It is also not necessary, since, if one is deeply fragmented, self-defeat, where the defeater and defeated are one and the same, may never occur. It is clear that rationality calls for the avoidance of informed self-defeating behavior and arguable that fragmentation into different selves over time does not itself open one up to criticism; indeed, insofar as some amount of unity is necessary for the attribution of self-defeat, deep fragmentation may make one less susceptible to criticism from the point of view of diachronic rationality. In any case, avoiding self-defeating behavior is consistent with radical transformation over time and the call to avoid self-defeating behavior is not a call for conservatism with respect to the values that define one's current self.

3
Instrumental Rationality Revamped

My reasoning in Chapters 1 and 2 suggests that instrumental rationality allows for certain forms of disorderliness, but requires that one proceed with caution and sometimes show restraint so as to avoid realizing a self-defeating pattern of behavior. In this chapter, I raise and solve a puzzle about this emerging conception of instrumental rationality. In a nutshell, the puzzle can be described as follows: Insofar as, from the point of view of instrumental rationality, showing restraint is a matter of settling on a dispreferred option, and realizing a self-defeating pattern of choice is a matter of realizing a dispreferred option, then showing restraint so as to avoid realizing a self-defeating pattern of choice amounts to settling on a dispreferred option so as to avoid realizing a dispreferred option, which doesn't make sense.

I solve this puzzle by distinguishing between *relational subjective appraisal responses* and *categorial subjective appraisal responses*, and interpreting these responses as figuring, in human psychology, as two distinct kinds of responses. Relational subjective appraisal responses rank options in relation to one another; it is these appraisal responses that are captured by the agent's preferences. (Recall that, as indicated in the introduction, I will be loosely describing the favoring of one option in a pair as the ranking of that option over the other—even when no ranking of all the options is to be had because the agent's preferences are cyclic.) By contrast, categorial subjective appraisal responses place options in categories, such as, for example, "great" or "terrible." While instrumental rationality is standardly understood as accountable to only relational subjective appraisal responses, I argue that it is also accountable

Choosing Well. Chrisoula Andreou, Oxford University Press. © Oxford University Press 2023.
DOI: 10.1093/oso/9780197584132.003.0004

to categorial subjective appraisal responses. If this is right, then we can make sense of the idea that, in cases involving rationally cyclic preferences, instrumental rationality sometimes calls for showing restraint so as to avoid realizing a self-defeating pattern of choice. For, when preferences are rationally cyclic, we can interpret "showing restraint" as "settling on a dispreferred option" and interpret the demand that one avoid realizing a self-defeating pattern of choice as requiring (perhaps among other things) not that one avoid realizing a dispreferred option, since that is not possible, but that one avoid ending up in an unnecessarily low appraisal category (e.g., ending up with a terrible option when great options are available). In the last section of Chapter 3, I raise and solve a similar puzzle regarding the money-pump argument. There I appeal to the idea that rationality requires one to avoid any alternative that is exactly the same as some other available alternative except for one disadvantageous difference.

3.1 A Puzzle about the Puzzle of the Self-Torturer

The puzzle I will focus on in this chapter is neatly illustrated by a careful analysis of Quinn's discussion of the puzzle of the self-torturer. Recall that, as indicated in my description of the puzzle in Section 1.1, for any two adjacent settings on the self-torturer's machine, n and $n+1$, the self-torturer cannot, with any confidence, distinguish between the settings just by the way he feels; but he gets $10,000 at each advance. As such, for any two settings n and $n+1$, the self-torturer prefers stopping at setting $n+1$ over stopping at setting n. And yet, the self-torturer also prefers stopping at setting zero, where he feels fine, over stopping at setting 1,000, where he feels excruciating pain. The self-torturer's preferences are thus cyclic; and yet, they seem perfectly understandable and indeed appropriate.

Significantly, Quinn's description of the case of the self-torturer suggests that the self-torturer is seeking to follow his reasons for action and that, for every setting zero to 1,000, there are no interferences that would stop the self-torturer from stopping at a particular setting if he were firmly convinced that he should stop there. The question is "What would the self-torturer do if he was (unwaveringly) fully rational?" The answer to this question depends, of course, on the correct theory of rationality, and we cannot, apart from a theory of rationality, rule out the self-torturer's stopping at any of the settings; in seeking to answer the question, we must, for every setting, treat stopping at that setting as an option available to the self-torturer. Importantly, to say that the answer to the question "What would the self-torturer do if he was fully rational?" depends on the correct theory of rationality is not to deny that our intuitions about plausible answers to the question can appropriately influence our views about whether a theory of rationality is correct.

According to Quinn (1993a), it is clear that, upon finding himself attached to the device, the self-torturer must, in order to take "reasonable advantage" of the opportunity he faces and ensure that he does not end up worse off than when he started, pick an appealing stopping point higher than setting zero but well short of setting 1,000 and then resolutely stick to his plan. Of course, if, given a decision to stop at a particular setting higher than setting zero but short of setting 1,000, the self-torturer will act accordingly, then, in deciding to stop at, say, setting n, the self-torturer is forgoing stopping at setting $n+1$, which he would prefer. The rationality of such a resolution is thus not acknowledged by the prevailing theory of instrumental rationality, which prohibits an agent from "forgo[ing] something that he would in fact prefer to get, all things considered" (1993a, 205). Quinn thus rejects the prevailing theory of instrumental rationality, which must, he suggests, be replaced by a theory that acknowledges the rationality of sometimes forming and following through on resolutions that selectively put aside certain preferences.

Presented somewhat more formally, the heart of Quinn's reasoning can be captured as follows:

P1: The self-torturer's cyclic preferences are rationally permissible.

P2: If the self-torturer's cyclic preferences are rationally permissible, then it is only insofar as rationality sometimes requires selectively putting aside certain preferences that rationally governéd choice can prompt the self-torturer to take reasonable advantage of the opportunity he faces, safely steering him clear of any alternative that is worse than the alternative he began with.

P3: One can count on rationally governed choice to prompt one to take reasonable advantage of opportunities one faces and, in doing so, to steer one clear of any alternative that is worse than the alternative one began with (at least if there are no unanticipated developments and one is not forced to deviate from the alternative one began with).

C: Rationality sometimes requires selectively putting aside certain preferences.

As Quinn anticipated, many have had qualms about P1. But even if Quinn is right about P1, and the theorists who oppose P1 are, as Quinn suggests, making things "too easy on [themselves]" and "too hard on the self-torturer" (1993a, 199), Quinn's reasoning seems problematic.

Notice first that, as Quinn makes explicit, his concern is with instrumental rationality. Moreover, putting aside complications he sees as irrelevant in relation to the puzzle of the self-torturer, he does not question, but instead adopts, the prevailing assumption that instrumental rationality "is and ought to be the slave of the agent's preferences" (1993a, 209).[1] But, in that case, it seems like the term "worse" in P3 must, for the sake of consistency, be interpreted as "worse in terms of serving the agent's preferences."[2] This, however, puts P3 in tension with Quinn's endorsement of resoluteness since, as Quinn understands resoluteness, it sometimes requires an agent to choose an alternative that serves his preferences worse than another available alternative. And if it is sometimes permissible to end up with an alternative that serves one's preferences worse than another available alternative, why would it not be permissible to end up with an alternative that serves one's preferences worse than the alternative with which one started? Relatedly, if it is rationally permissible to make a series of choices that leads one to an alternative that is worse than another alternative that one could have opted for, why would it matter whether the other alternative is the alternative one began with, an alternative that was available after one took some further steps, or an alternative that would be available if one continued to proceed?[3]

Consider, by way of illustration, the following case: Suppose that one has access to five cups of tea. The leftmost tea (tea1) is very hot but not very flavorful, and the rest are such that each is more flavorful but not quite as hot as the one just to the left of it; tea5, on

---

[1] In "Putting Rationality in its Place," Quinn suggests that instrumental rationality is "mere cleverness" and not a "real virtue" of practical rationality if one's practical reasoning is not constrained by good ends (1993b, 234).

[2] Interestingly, Quinn, at one point, maintains that "better than . . . is transitive" (1993a, 199), where "better than" qualifies as transitive if, for all X, Y, and Z, if X is better than Y and Y is better than Z, then X is better than Z. But, if "better than" is understood as (something like) "better in terms of serving the agent's preferences," it is not clear that Quinn is entitled to maintain that "better than" is transitive while also maintaining that the self-torturer's preferences are genuinely and rationally cyclic. And if "better than" is not understood in terms of the agent's preferences, it is not clear that Quinn is entitled to assume that the relation is relevant to instrumental rationality, given his adoption of the prevailing assumption that instrumental rationality "is and ought to be the slave of the agent's preferences" (209). I consider the question of what we should conclude about the (presumed) acyclicity of the "better than" relation if rational preferences can be cyclic in Chapter 6.

[3] This question needs to be considered even if it is granted that, "*intuitively*," it seems "clear" that "in the case of the self-torturer, . . . a reasonable decision rule should select only settings preferred to 0" (Carlson 1996, emphasis mine).

the far right, is very flavorful but also lukewarm. Suppose further that one's preferences over the cups of tea (taking into account both temperature and flavor) are cyclic, with tea2 preferred to tea1, tea3 preferred to tea2, tea4 preferred to tea3, tea5 preferred to tea4, but tea1 preferred to tea5. Suppose also that these cyclic preferences are rationally permissible. Now assume that one does not possess any of the teas and that (as per Quinn's suggestion that, given rationally permissible cyclic preferences, it is rationally permissible to make a series of choices that leads one to an alternative that serves one's preferences worse than another alternative that one could have opted for) selecting teaN is rationally permissible even though teaN serves one's preferences worse than teaM. Why should the permissibility of selecting teaN change if, instead of it being the case that one never previously possessed any of the teas, the scenario is such that one was initially given teaM? In both scenarios, one selects teaN even though teaM is available. Why should the fact that one was initially given teaM change the permissibility of ending up with teaN?

My point, in short, is that, as soon as one grants that, in cases like the case of the self-torturer, it is rationally permissible, and indeed rationally required, that one stick with an option even though it serves one's preferences worse than another available alternative, then it seems ad hoc to insist that rationality does not permit a series of choices that leads one to an option that serves one's preferences worse than the alternative one began with.[4]

---

[4] In "Intransitive Preferences, Vagueness, and the Structure of Procrastination," Duncan MacIntosh argues that "if the self-torturer really has intransitive preferences . . . he rationally should proceed to the maximum level" (2010, 73). Relatedly, he claims that, for an agent with intransitive preferences,

> each position he could have been in is such that if he does not move to a different position, he is pair-wise worse off. So, he would have been irrational to stay where he was. In moving, he has not made himself any worse off than he was before. (76)

I disagree with MacIntosh's reasoning, but my concerns about Quinn's take on the puzzle of the self-torturer have been influenced by MacIntosh's thought-provoking challenges concerning the assumed irrationality of the self-torturer's proceeding to 1,000.

3.2 The Real Puzzle of the Self-Torturer

What shall we say, then, about the case of the self-torturer? Well, if we grant, as I do, that it is rationally permissible for the self-torturer to end up with an alternative that serves his preferences worse than some other alternative he could have opted for, then, given my reasoning in the previous section, we cannot just assume that rationality prohibits the self-torturer from making a series of choices that leads to an alternative that serves his preferences worse than the alternative he began with.[5] But then we've lost our apparent reason for thinking there is something irrational about the self-torturer's proceeding at each point and thus going to 1,000.[6] And this is puzzling, since, intuitively, there is something irrational about the self-torturer's proceeding at each point and thus going to 1,000. I turn now to identifying where the irrationality in this scenario lies. (As will become apparent, one can identify where the irrationality in this scenario lies, without pinpointing or even supposing that there is a specific setting at which the self-torturer rationally should stop. There may instead be a fuzzily bounded range of rationally acceptable stopping points, with no clear first rationally unacceptable stopping point. I say more concerning the presumed vagueness in the self-torturer's situation below.)

Here, in a nutshell, is the answer: The irrationality lies not in the fact that the self-torturer ends up with an alternative that serves his

---

[5] Insofar as cyclic preferences can be rational, Quinn's suggestion that it is rationally permissible for the self-torturer to end up with an alternative that serves his preferences worse than some other alternative he could have opted for, which I will discuss below in Section 3.3, accords with the *practicability assumption* that will be discussed in Chapter 6. According to the practicability assumption, rationality cannot be such that, even without having made any prior errors, one can be in a predicament wherein every option is rationally inadvisable. This assumption fits neatly with the idea that rationality cannot issue a set of demands or recommendations regarding choosing among the available alternatives that one cannot, even in principle, follow, no matter how perfectly one has been proceeding.

[6] Keep in mind that since the self-torturer's preferences are cyclic, we cannot say that his going to 1,000 appears far lower in his ranking of his options (and is in this sense much less preferred) than the option of stopping at zero.

preferences worse than the one he started with, but that (although unimpaired by any lack of information about his situation) the self-torturer ends up with a terrible alternative when non-terrible alternatives are available. Now to explain.

My explanation relies on a distinction that is drawn from David Papineau's work on color perception—the distinction is between *categorical responses* and *relational responses*. Note that while I will, in the following brief review of Papineau's work on color responses, stick with the term "categorical," I will, for a reason that will be explained below, switch to the term "categorial" once I start applying his distinction to appraisal responses.

In "Can We Really See a Million Colours?" David Papineau (2015) argues that "our conscious colour experience is the joint product of two different kinds of perceptual state" (277): via one state, we have *categorical* color responses, wherein we experience a surface as of a certain color, say cN, where cN is among the finite set of distinct conscious visual color experiences $\{c1, c2, c3, \ldots, cS\}$ the perceiver can have; via the other state, we have *relational* color responses, wherein we experience adjacent color samples as either the same or as in some way different from one another.[7] As Papineau explains, his position has interesting implications concerning the interpretation of color discrimination data. Consider, for example, the view that "human beings are capable of well over a million different conscious visual responses to coloured surfaces" (274). This view is based on (1) evidence that, when comparing pairs of color

---

[7] Diana Raffman (1994) raises this possibility and uses the distinction to argue that two color patches that are seen as belonging to different categories when judged singly can be seen as belonging to the same category when judged pairwise. This is in turn used to "explain, in an *intuitively* compelling way, how a difference in kind can obtain between the endpoints (among others) of an effectively continuous series" and thus resolve the paradox in sorites cases (43). Quinn's puzzle incorporates the assumption that, whatever the explanation, a difference in kind can obtain between the endpoints of an effectively continuous series. (More specifically, Quinn assumes that someone can go from no pain to excruciating pain via a series of unnoticeable or barely noticeable differences.) I will make the same assumption without committing to any particular explanation (although I do find Raffman's explanation plausible).

samples, humans can consciously register color differences between more than a million different samples, and (2) the assumption that "our consciously registering a *difference in colour* must derive from our first having *one* colour response to the left-hand side surface, and *another* colour response to the right-hand [side] surface, and thence registering that there is a difference" (274). But if, as Papineau argues, "the detection of colour differences between adjacent surfaces does not [always] derive from prior [independent] responses to each surface, there is no need to posit a million such responses to account for the discrimination data" (275). For there is then room for the visual system to issue "a relational judgement that two adjacent samples . . . *differ* even in cases where the two surfaces produce [the *same* conscious visual experience, and so] the *same* categorical colour response [when viewed each on its own]" (278); moreover, there is, as Papineau makes clear, room for the possibility that one's conscious visual experience when viewing one pair of color samples, say, sample orange_{23} next to sample orange_{24}, can be the same as one's conscious visual experience when viewing a different pair of samples, say sample orange_{27} next to sample orange_{28}.

As Papineau emphasizes, it is "entirely consistent" with his view that categorical color responses can vary from person to person (2015, 276). Whereas I might have the same conscious visual experience when I view color sample 2 (by itself) and when I view color sample 3 (by itself), you might have a different conscious visual experience when you view color sample 2 (by itself) than you have when you view color sample 3 (by itself). There is certainly room for

variations in culture, training, and natural endowment [to] make a significant difference to the repertoire of [categorical] colour responses available to different individuals. Maybe some individuals are . . . only capable of a few dozen such responses, while others—painters or interior decorators, say—are capable of many hundreds. (276)

Whether Papineau's position concerning color perception is correct is not something we can or need to take up here. What is important for my purposes is that Papineau's distinction between categorical responses and relational responses, or rather, the related distinction between *categorial appraisal responses* and *relational appraisal responses*, can—if the responses are understood as figuring, in human psychology, as two distinct kinds of responses—illuminate the nature of instrumental rationality and the puzzle of the self-torturer. Note that I'm here switching from "categorical" to "categorial" because, with respect to appraisal responses, "categorical" strongly suggests objective appraisal responses (of the sort associated with Kant's "categorical imperative"), which is not a connotation that I want here, since the categorial appraisal responses I have in mind can be subjective. More on this shortly.

Notice first that in appraising an alternative, I might respond *categorially* with something like "X is terrible," or I might respond *relationally* with something like "X is worse than Y." The first sort of response is *categorial* in the sense that it indicates the appraisal category that I see X as falling in. The second sort of response provides no such category information. To appraise X as worse than Y leaves completely open the question of what category I place X in on the spectrum from, say, terrible to fantastic. It indicates only how I appraise X and Y in relation to each other.[8]

As indicated above, in the sense of interest here, to say that a response is a categorial appraisal response is not to say that it is or purports to be objective. My appraisal of the taste of vegemite as terrible counts as a categorial appraisal response even though my appraisal is, I grant, thoroughly subjective. Note also that, in the

---

[8] Note that, although in the case of the self-torturer, the focus is on the consequences of the available alternatives, there is nothing in the idea of an appraisal response that requires that appraisal responses to potential actions be consequence-oriented; relatedly, there is, for all I say here, room for appraising an action as terrible even if it does not have terrible consequences.

sense of interest here, to say that a response is a categorial appraisal response is not to say that there were no comparisons or contrasts in play when the response occurred. I might find a piece of chocolate terrible-tasting because I am used to very high-end chocolate. Still, "this chocolate tastes terrible" says something about where I place (the taste of) this chocolate on the spectrum from, say, terrible to fantastic (and so about whether my culinary experience is positive, negative, or neutral); the judgment "this chocolate tastes worse than the chocolate I had yesterday" does not, in itself, provide any such information.

As in the color case, once one distinguishes between categorial and relational responses, there is room for scenarios such as the following: L is capable of both categorial responses and relational responses with respect to appraisals of a particular type in a particular domain or over a particular set of options; the number of distinct categorial responses L has along the most refined spectrum of categorial responses available to L for appraisals of the relevant type in the relevant domain or over the relevant options is finite; and, even when L uses the most refined spectrum of categorial responses available to them for appraisals of the relevant type in the relevant domain or over the relevant options, L sometimes has relational responses that prompt them to discriminate between alternatives that they have the same categorial response to when they consider each on its own. To take a concrete case, there is room for scenarios such as the following: L is capable of categorial and relational responses concerning the goodness (to L) of various samples of chocolate; the set {terrible, very bad, bad, fair, good, great, fantastic} figures as the most refined spectrum of L's categorial appraisal responses concerning the goodness (to L) of various samples of chocolate; in considering two chocolate samples, say A and B, L has the same categorial appraisal response when L considers each on its own, and yet L also has a relational response of the form "A is worse than B." As Papineau emphasizes, there is no guarantee that our categorial responses and our relational responses will prompt the same discriminations.[9]

Note that to say that the number of distinct categorial appraisal responses that an agent has in a particular domain or over a particular set of options is finite is not to say that every alternative the agent considers will fall squarely into one appraisal category or another. The possibility of vagueness, understood as involving fuzzy boundaries, is by no means ruled out. Given the possibility of vagueness, a preference cycle (such as the self-torturer's) can transition, over a *series* of options that are adjacent to one another in the cycle, from one option to another that is determinately in a lower (appraisal) category without there being any single pair of adjacent options in the cycle such that one option is determinately in a lower category than the next. Note, relatedly, that I am not committed to the idea that relational appraisal responses and categorical appraisal responses will ever pull in different directions in relation to two options that fall squarely in different leagues or categories (such as "fair" and "bad"); indeed, I am happy to grant that if, for instance, an agent appraises one option as fair and another as bad, they are sure to prefer the former; what I am suggesting is that relational appraisal responses and categorical appraisal responses can pull in different directions over a *series* of options that span a set of vaguely bounded leagues or categories.

My discussion so far suggests that, if an agent's preferences are cyclic, one should not expect to find a thoroughly tidy relation between the agent's categorial appraisal responses to the alternatives she faces and the agent's relational appraisal responses to the alternatives she faces; or at least this is so if (1) it is the agent's relational appraisal responses that are captured by her preferences, and (2) the categorial responses that are relevant in the case at hand, even if they are complicated by vagueness, involve categories

[9] I say more about this and consider potential objections in the next chapter, which incorporates a version of Andreou (2015b).

that can be arranged from lowest to highest (as with the categories "terrible," "very bad," "bad," "fair," "good," "great," "fantastic"). However, it might be claimed that if an agent's preferences over a set of options are cyclic, then the only categorial responses the agent can have to the options will be such that the relevant categories cannot be arranged from lowest to highest, but instead form a loop. The case of the self-torturer speaks against this view. Although the self-torturer's preferences over his options are cyclic, the self-torturer can and does have categorial responses like "that would be a terrible result" and "that would be a fantastic result"; and he does *not* see the spectrum from "terrible" to "fantastic" as forming a loop so that talk of higher and lower appraisal categories is out of place—to the contrary, it is precisely because talk of higher and lower appraisal categories seems perfectly in order in the case of the self-torturer that it is plausible to suggest that the self-torturer should not end up with options in some of the available categories. (More on this below.) If the case of the self-torturer were such that talk of higher and lower appraisal categories were out of place, it is far from clear that we could substantiate the claim that some of the options in the case ought to be avoided. It is the combination of cyclic preferences and non-cyclic categories that makes the case particularly interesting.

It might be suggested that, insofar as the categories associated with a set of categorial responses can be arranged from lowest to highest, we can say that the agent has preferences over the categories, and that *these* preferences are not cyclic. For example, in the case of the self-torturer, we can say that the self-torturer has preferences over the categories in the spectrum from "terrible" to "fantastic," and that *these* preferences are not cyclic. I will not here delve into this suggestion. I want only to emphasize that it in no way undermines the idea that the self-torturer's pairwise preferences between the options he actually faces are cyclic. Moreover, it does not support the idea that *all* the self-torturer's subjective appraisal responses are preferences (understood as subjective *relational* appraisal responses). To say that the self-torturer prefers the category "fantastic" to the category "terrible" is to say that the self-torturer prefers options to which he has the subjective categorial appraisal response "this is fantastic" over options to which he has the subjective categorial appraisal response "this is terrible"; subjective *categorial* appraisal responses (and the valences they convey) remain in play.

Now consider the following proposal, which is related to P3 (in my reconstruction of Quinn's reasoning):

> P3*: One can count on rationally governed choice to steer one away from any alternative that is (determinately) in a lower appraisal category than another available alternative (at least if there are no unanticipated developments and the set of appraisal categories is finite).

Notice that P3* applies only when talk of higher and lower categories is in order, and so only when the categories in play do not form a loop.

P3* is, I think, quite plausible and it can accommodate the idea that it is rationally impermissible for the self-torturer to end up at 1,000 without dismissing the self-torturer's cyclic preferences as rationally impermissible. Some might see P3* as going further out on a limb than is necessary relative to the case of the self-torturer, and favor instead the following more modest proposal:

> P3′: One can count on rationally governed choice to steer one away from a terrible alternative when an alternative that is (determinately) in a higher appraisal category is available.[10]

---

[10] Thanks to Sarah Stroud for pointing out that I could make do with this more modest proposal.

I should thus note that, while I will focus on P3*, the gist of my rea-soning below holds even if P3* is replaced with P3ʹ (and P2* in the argument below is altered accordingly).

Insofar as rational cyclic preferences are possible, P3* implies that instrumental rationality sometimes requires selectively putting aside certain preferences, even if these preferences are rationally permis-sible. (Note that P3* is consistent with the possibility that rationality allows the agent to use her discretion in terms of deciding where ex-actly to deviate from her preferences, so long as the result conforms to P3*.) Preferences are relational responses. If the self-torturer had nothing but the relational responses that Quinn describes and these responses were rationally permissible, then there would be no way to show that it is irrational for the self-torturer to end up at 1,000. But the self-torturer's subjective appraisal responses also include appraisal responses of the form "alternative X is terrible," and in-strumental rationality is also accountable to these responses. From here, we can get to an internally consistent argument that fits with the spirit of Quinn's resolution of the puzzle of the self-torturer, al-though Quinn himself failed to properly identify the problem or a viable resolution. The argument is as follows:

P1: The self-torturer's cyclic preferences are rationally permissible.

P2*: If the self-torturer's cyclic preferences are rationally permis-sible, then it is only insofar as rationality requires selectively put-ting aside certain preferences/relational appraisal responses that rationally governed choice can steer the self-torturer away from any alternative that is in a lower appraisal category than another available alternative.

P3*: One can count on rationally governed choice to steer one away from any alternative that is in a lower appraisal category than another available alternative (at least if there are no unantic-ipated developments and the set of appraisal categories is finite).

C*: Rationality sometimes requires selectively putting aside certain preferences.

In the case of the self-torturer, the agent's categorial appraisal responses are such that some alternatives count as terrible and some do not—indeed, some may count as good, great, or even fantastic. As such, it is not rationally permissible for the self-torturer to end up with a terrible alternative. Notice that it need not be that, in all cases of cyclic preferences, the agent's categorial appraisal responses to the available alternatives fall in different categories. Since relational responses can prompt discriminations that are not prompted by the agent's categorial responses, it may be that an agent's relational responses to a set of alternatives reflect cyclic preferences even though her categorial responses place them all in the same category, say "fair." Recall the tea case, wherein the leftmost tea (tea1) is very hot but not very flavorful, and the rest are such that each is more flavorful but not quite as hot as the one just to the left of it; tea5, on the far right, is very flavorful but also lukewarm. It may be that the agent's preferences over the teas are cyclic even though the agent counts all the teas as fair. If so, and if the cyclic preferences are rationally permissible, then we can see why it can be rationally permissible for her to end up with any of the teas, and why it doesn't matter which one she started with. Given that the agent's preferences over the teas are rationally cyclic, instrumental rationality cannot forbid the agent from ending up with a tea that is dispreferred to another available tea; it *can* forbid the agent from ending up with a tea that falls in a lower category than another available tea, but when all the teas fall in the same category, this won't occur no matter which tea she ends up with.

Notice that my reasoning leaves room for the possibility that, when an agent's preferences over a set of options are not cyclic, rationality may, in that case, require that the agent act on her relational responses/preferences regarding the options among which she must currently choose, even if she has the *same* categorial response to all the options. As such, it does not follow from my reasoning that an agent need only attend to her categorial appraisal responses.

3.3 Rational Dilemmas

Note that, in rethinking Quinn's argument, I have granted that, insofar as an agent's preferences are rationally cyclic, it is rationally permissible for the agent to end up with an alternative that serves their preferences worse than some other alternative they could have opted for. But it might be suggested that this neglects the possibility that an agent whose preferences are rationally cyclic faces a rational dilemma.

My response to this concern varies depending on what sort of rational dilemma is supposed to be in play. According to a very weak sense of "rational dilemma," an agent faces a rational dilemma if, whatever she chooses, it makes sense for her to experience rational regret, where this involves rationally mourning the loss of a forgone good. Although I have not yet discussed such mourning, there is, as will become clear in Chapter 8, no tension between acknowledging this sort of dilemma while embracing everything I have said so far. Indeed, I do just that.

There is, however, a stronger sense of "rational dilemma" according to which to be in a rational dilemma is to be in a situation in which every option is rationally impermissible; and the claim that an agent with rationally cyclic preferences faces a rational dilemma in this sense is one that I do resist, in part so that the distinction between rationally permissible options and rationally impermissible options can function, as it ideally should, as the crucial action-guiding distinction for a rational agent. Although delving into my reasons for resistance, which are discussed in Andreou (2019c), would take me too far afield, I will here briefly flag what I see as a crucial thing to consider. Given rationally cyclic preferences, there are two alternatives: one can maintain that, because every option is dominated by another available option, every option must be dismissed as rationally impermissible; or one can maintain that, because every option is dominated by another available option, the consideration that an option is dominated by another available option is not a conclusive reason against the option. If one opts for the first alternative, then, in the case of the self-torturer, both of the following must be dismissed as impermissible, even if the self-torturer's preferences are rational: (1) settling on an option in the lowest appraisal category (which might be "terrible" and include the option "stopping at setting 999"); and (2) settling on an option in the highest available appraisal category (which might be "fantastic" and include the option "stopping at setting 15"). But (1) can clearly be dismissed as rationally misguided in a way that the (2) cannot. This crucial bit of guidance is obscured by the dismissal of both options as impermissible. It thus seems sensible to conclude that the sense in which (2) is impermissible, if there is any such sense, is not the sense that matters when one is trying to figure out what to do.

3.4 The Moral Regarding
Instrumental Rationality

The traditional conception of instrumental rationality combines the idea that instrumental rationality is grounded in our subjective appraisal responses with the assumption that our preferences, understood as relational appraisal responses, exhaust our subjective appraisal responses; but, in addition to our relational appraisal responses, we have subjective categorial appraisal responses. It is precisely when the latter responses are in play that it can be irrational to end up with some alternatives but not others even if one's preferences are rationally cyclic. Without categorial appraisal responses, any alternative in a preference loop with a spectrum of options like the one in the case of the self-torturer would be just as rationally permissible as any other. With categorial appraisal responses, this need not be so. Relatedly, for some alternatives, ending up with that alternative can be rationally impermissible regardless of whether or not the alternative serves the agent's preferences worse than the one that the agent started with or whether or not the agent ended up there as a result of deviating from a prior plan; it can be impermissible because it is in a lower appraisal category than another alternative that the agent could have opted for. The moral, in short, is that the subjective responses that instrumental rationality is responsive and accountable to are not just the agent's preferences. Our subjective responses also include appraisals that do not qualify as relational in the relevant sense—appraisals associated with a rational requirement (P3*) that can, in theory and in practice, justify selectively putting aside certain preferences.

3.5 Making Sense of the Money-Pump Argument

The puzzle I raised and solved in the preceding sections of this chapter is closely related to a puzzle regarding the money-pump argument. The puzzle is as follows: According to a prominent interpretation of the money-pump argument, the argument is supposed to show that cyclic preferences are irrational by showing that following one's cyclic preferences can lead one to a dispreferred alternative (more on this below). But then the argument is grounded in the *assumption* that it is irrational to make choices that lead one to a dispreferred alternative; and, as I explain, this assumption arguably begs the question against someone who thinks rational preference cycles are possible. The assumption that it is irrational to make choices that lead one to a dispreferred alternative is also problematic in relation to the reinterpretation of the money-pump argument presented in Chapter 1, which allows for rationally cyclic preferences and casts the threat of being money pumped as undermining the idea that a rational agent will invariably act on their preferences. For, if one allows for rationally cyclic preferences, then one must grant that even a rational agent can be in a position where they must settle on a dispreferred alternative. But then it cannot be assumed that it is irrational to make choices that lead one to a dispreferred alternative. The solution is to see the money-pump argument as relying on an assumption that is common ground between opponents and defenders of rationally cyclic preferences, namely the assumption that rationality requires one to avoid any alternative that is exactly the same as some other available alternative except for one disadvantageous difference. Interpreted in this way, the argument is reestablished as forcefully suggesting that either rational preferences cannot be cyclic or rational agents do not invariably follow their preferences.

As explained in Chapter 1, the money-pump argument is supposed to establish that an agent with cyclic preferences is irrational because she is susceptible to being money pumped. Suppose, to return to an earlier example, that A has the choice between five cups of tea: the leftmost tea (tea1) is very hot but not very flavorful, and the rest are such that each is more flavorful but not quite as hot as the one just to the left of it; tea5, on the far right, is very flavorful but also lukewarm. A could easily find that her preferences over the cups of tea (taking into account both temperature and flavor) are cyclic, with tea2 preferred to tea1, tea3 preferred to tea2, tea4 preferred to tea3, tea5 preferred to tea4, but tea1 preferred to tea5. Now suppose also that A has some money; that, other things equal, A prefers having more money to less; and that there is a small amount of money, say a penny, such that for all X and Y such that A prefers teaX to teaY, she also prefers teaX and a charge of a penny to teaY. Suppose finally that A has tea1. A can be money pumped as follows: Given her preferences, A will be willing to pay a penny to trade tea1 for tea2; similarly, she will be willing to pay a penny to trade tea2 for tea3, and then another penny to trade tea3 for tea4, and then another penny to trade tea4 for tea5, and then another penny to trade tea5 for tea1. Her preferences will thus prompt her to accept a series of trades that lead her to tea1 (which is the tea she had to begin with) and five less pennies than she started with. And, given further trading opportunities, she is liable to end up with tea1 and no money at all.

Some responses to the money-pump argument have focused on challenging the idea that agents with cyclic preferences are as susceptible to being money pumped as the money-pump argument suggests.[11] The worry I want to consider here—and attempt to address shortly—is quite different. It is that, even if agents with cyclic preferences are as susceptible to being money pumped as the money-pump argument suggests, the argument is unacceptable because it is question-begging and pointlessly distracting.

Consider the query "What is (supposed to be) irrational about being money pumped (assuming the agent prefers more money to less)?" A prominent view in the follow-up literature that explicitly considers this question is that the money-pump argument is to be understood in terms of the following response (which, in the spirit of instrumentalism, is consistent with counting susceptibility to financial exploitation or to a sure financial loss as problematic only insofar as it conflicts with the agent's preferences): in cases where an agent who prefers more money to less is money pumped, they choose in a way that realizes a dispreferred or "dominated" alternative, understood as "an alternative to which another is preferred"

---

[11] See, for example, Frederic Schick's influential response in Schick (1986). I develop a related position in Andreou (2007a). See also McClennen (1990). More recently, Johanna Thoma (in her "Preference Cycles and the Requirements of Instrumental Rationality," unpublished) has suggested that the money pump argument "relies on a fatal equivocation about the standard of instrumental rationality," and that when this is recognized it becomes clear that either "we cannot show that instrumentally rational agents must adopt acyclical preferences to avoid being money-pumped" or "we cannot show that being money-pumped is instrumentally irrational."

(Gustafsson 2013, 462);[12] the agent thus deprives themselves of a preferred alternative, which is irrational. Note that, in accordance with common usage, the notion of deprivation in play here does not require that one have the preferred alternative to begin with. For instance, given that A prefers tea2 to tea1, A would count as depriving herself of a preferred alternative even if she started with nothing and ended up with tea1 via a direct selection from the set {tea1, tea2}; similarly, A would count as depriving herself of a preferred alternative even if A started with tea1 and stuck with this alternative over tea2.

If the money-pump argument is understood in terms of the preceding response, then it emerges as question-begging. To see this, consider the following inquiry:

Q: Is it irrational to choose in a way that realizes an alternative to which another is preferred (assuming that, as in the cases of interest, there are no unmentioned complications, such as, for instance, a change of preferences or infinitely many alternatives)?

If it is not assumed that cyclic preferences are irrational, then it is plausible to reply as follows:

R: Maybe not. If there are situations in which an agent's preferences over the options are cyclic, and these cyclic preferences cannot be dismissed as irrational, then, in these situations, it is rationally permissible to choose in a way that realizes an alternative to which another is preferred, since, when an agent's preferences

[12] Johan Gustafsson's related reasoning regarding the money-pump argument is touched on in note 14 below. See also, for example, Levi (2002), wherein Isaac Levi characterizes money-pump arguments as "designed" to show that individuals who violate "acyclicity of preference" will "end up choosing options that are dominated by other options available to them" (S241–S242).

over the options are cyclic, *every* alternative is one to which another is preferred.[13]

The answer to Q thus depends on whether cyclic preferences are irrational. As such, while it may be tempting to assume that it is irrational to make choices that lead one to a dispreferred alternative, if the money-pump argument is grounded in this assumption (or intuition), the argument is question-begging. While it might seem obvious to the proponent of the money-pump argument that it is irrational to make choices that lead one to a dispreferred alternative, it might seem just as obvious to defenders of cyclic preferences that there are cases of rationally permissible cyclic preferences that serve as clear counterexamples to this loaded starting point.

A related concern is that if it could be assumed that it is irrational to choose in a way that realizes an alternative to which another is preferred, the money-pump argument would be a complicated distraction in the debate concerning cyclic preferences. For, given that assumption, one would not need to appeal to a susceptibility to being money pumped to conclude that cyclic preferences are irrational. One could simply point out that, even if there is no threat of being money pumped, an agent with cyclic preferences will end up with an alternative to which another is preferred.[14]

As indicated above, the assumption that it is irrational to make choices that lead one to a dispreferred alternative is also problematic in relation to the reinterpretation of the money-pump

---

[13] This assumes that rationally uncriticizable agents will not face rational dilemmas in which every alternative is rationally impermissible. If, by contrast, such agents can face such dilemmas, then even a conclusive demonstration that an agent with cyclic preferences will wind up with a rationally impermissible alternative would not establish the irrationality of cyclic preferences.

[14] Gustafsson (2013) seems to recognize this, but not as a reason to seek a more charitable interpretation of the money-pump argument; instead, he sees it as a reason to favor the "more direct synchronic argument" that zeros in on the idea that that it is irrational to choose in a way that realizes a dispreferred alternative. But, as we have seen, if the money-pump argument is interpreted as relying on this idea, it emerges as question-begging, and this adds to the case for seeking a more charitable interpretation.

argument presented in Chapter 1, which allows for rationally cyclic preferences and casts the threat of being money pumped as undermining the idea that a rational agent will invariably act on her preferences. For, if one allows for rationally cyclic preferences, then one must grant that even a rational agent can be in a position where she must settle on a dispreferred alternative. But then it cannot be assumed that it is irrational to make choices that lead one to a dispreferred alternative.

If we are to avoid the conclusion that the money-pump argument is seriously problematic, the claim that it is irrational for, say, A to end up with tea1 and five less pennies than she started with (henceforth tea1$^{\downarrow 5¢}$) must appeal to a weaker assumption (or intuition) than the assumption that it is irrational to choose in a way that realizes an alternative to which another is preferred. Here is a weaker assumption that accommodates and generalizes the idea that it is irrational for A to end up with tea1$^{\downarrow 5¢}$:

P: It is irrational to make a choice or series of choices that leads one to an alternative Y which is such that Y is identical to another alternative X except with respect to one dimension of concern and, in that respect, Y is dispreferred to X.[15]

Less formally, P essentially requires that one avoid any alternative that is exactly the same as some other available alternative except for one disadvantageous difference. (According to a plausible generalization of P, one should avoid any alternative that is exactly

---

[15] For some related discussion regarding accommodating "the intuitive irrationality of being money-pumped," see Thoma's "Preference Cycles and the Requirements of Instrumental Rationality" (unpublished), wherein Thoma (1) argues that the intuition does not fit with the most prominent candidate for "the standard of instrumental rationality," and (2) offers an alternative candidate and an adapted version of P (citing Andreou [2016], which is where I originally formulated P). Although delving into Thoma's reasoning would take me too far afield, it is worth noting that, although our revisionary conceptions of instrumental rationality differ, both my conception and Thoma's conception allow for instrumentally rational counter-preferential choice.

the same as some other available alternative except for x disadvantageous difference(s), where x is greater or equal to 1.)

P (modulo some qualifications and restrictions that have been left implicit since they are not pertinent in relation to standard money-pump cases) can plausibly be cast as at the core of the money-pump argument (be it the original version or the reinterpretation presented in Chapter 1). And P does not beg the question against defenders of cyclic preferences. For, even defenders of cyclic preferences can grant that, when the alternatives that A will face include tea1, tea2$^{\downarrow 1¢}$, tea3$^{\downarrow 2¢}$, tea4$^{\downarrow 3¢}$, tea5$^{\downarrow 4¢}$, and tea1$^{\downarrow 5¢}$, realizing any of the first five options may be acceptable, but realizing the last option is not. Indeed, the fact that some of the most prominent defenders of cyclic preferences have focused on challenging the idea that an agent with cyclic preferences is particularly susceptible to being money pumped suggests that they accept (something like) P.

In short, given either the traditional version of the money-pump argument or the reinterpretation presented in Chapter 1 (which I favor), there is strong reason to resist understanding the argument as grounded in the assumption (or intuition) that it is irrational to choose in a way that realizes an alternative to which another is preferred; that interpretation makes the "argument" seem boldly question-begging, purely distracting, or otherwise seriously problematic, and there is an alternative interpretation that is more promising. Of course, since the alternative interpretation is compatible with the idea that what the argument establishes is that *either* cyclic preferences are irrational *or* it is sometimes rational to settle on a dispreferred alternative, even the more promising version of the argument developed in this section does not amount to an argument against rationally cyclic preferences.

4

Parity

In Section 3.2 of the preceding chapter, I introduced the distinction between relational and categorial subjective appraisal responses and showed how it illuminates the possibility of rationally cyclic preferences. In this chapter, I return to the distinction and use it to illuminate the possibility of incommensurable alternatives and incomplete preferences. In particular, I show how it allows us to make sense of the possibility of two options not being one better than the other or exactly equally good, but still comparable as "on a par." This possibility reinforces the possibility of rationally incomplete preferences.

4.1 Parity Illuminated

Let us begin by returning to Chang's coffee and tea case. An agent tastes A, a cup of Jasmine tea, and B, a cup of Sumatra Gold coffee, and determines, in accordance with her sensibility, that neither one tastes better than the other. Now a second, slightly more fragrant cup of Jasmine tea, A+, is introduced and the agent determines, in accordance with her sensibility, that it tastes better than the original tea but not better than the original coffee. Moreover, in the case at hand, all that matters is which drink tastes better to her; there is nothing else at stake. This seems like a particularly simple and compelling case in which (relative to what matters in the case at hand) A is not better than B, and B is not better than A, and yet A and B do not qualify as exactly equally good because A+ is better than A but not better than B.

Choosing Well. Chrisoula Andreou, Oxford University Press. © Oxford University Press 2023.
DOI: 10.1093/oso/9780197584132.003.0005

For Chang, even if, as she believes, this is right, it does not follow that A and B are incomparable (in terms of how valuable they are overall relative to what matters, from the point of view of practical reason, in the case at hand). This would follow if the *trichotomy thesis* were correct. According to the trichotomy thesis, "the conceptual space of comparability between two items is spanned by the trichotomy of relations 'better than,' 'worse than,' and 'equally good': if none of those relations holds, the items are incomparable" (Chang 2002a, 661). But, according to Chang, two options that are not *trichotomously comparable* (i.e., comparable in terms of the preceding trichotomy of relations) may still be comparable as "on a par."[1] But what is the (purported) positive relation in play here?

In this section, I will show how the distinction between relational and categorial appraisal responses can illuminate what is going on in cases like Chang's coffee and tea case in a way that supports the possibility of two options not being trichotomously comparable but still being comparable as "on a par." As will become apparent, I will do this not by providing a general account of parity, but by bringing out a positive relation tied to categorial appraisal responses that can ground the claim of parity in cases like Chang's coffee or tea case. Later in the chapter, I will show how my reasoning might be extended to ground the claim of parity in other types of cases. In the next chapter, complications associated with comparing options constituted by combinations of positive and negative features that are not conducive to overall categorial appraisal responses will emerge and be addressed.

First some clarificatory remarks. It might be supposed (as is suggested in Chang's work on parity)[2] that the conception of parity we are after is actually such that two options can count as on a par only if they are not comparable as one better than the other or as

---

[1] For some related discussion regarding options that are "in the same league" or "roughly equal," see, for example, Parfit (1984, 431) and Griffin (1986, 96–97).

[2] See, for example, Chang (1997).

exactly equally good. As will become apparent, my reasoning will not rely on or push me to this idea, but it will leave room for understanding parity in this way. For now, I will assume only that the conception of parity we are after is such that parity involves a positive relation that can obtain in the absence of trichotomous comparability, and I will focus, to begin with, on substantiating the possibility of such a relation.

Turn now to an interpretation of parity that should be distinguished from the one at issue here:[3] Two options, say A and B, might be counted as on a par if and only if the range of permissible attitudes toward the options is such that it is rationally permissible to prefer A to B but also rationally permissible to prefer B to A.[4] Suppose, to return to the beverages in Chang's case, that, where taste is all that is at stake, it is rationally permissible to prefer the coffee over the (original) tea, but also rationally permissible to prefer the tea over the coffee. Then, according to the interpretation of parity just referenced, the two beverages count as on a par. This is certainly a defensible way of using "on a par," but according to the notion of parity that is of central interest in the current inquiry—which is focused on overall evaluations that are relative to all that matters in the case at hand, which can include the preferences of the choosing agent—even if it is rationally permissible to prefer the coffee over the tea and rationally permissible to prefer the tea over the coffee, the coffee and the tea may be on a par for one agent, such

---

[3] See Qizilbash (2018) for a related distinction between "two parity views." Qizilbash's distinction is between the "rough equality view" and the "fitting attitudes view." As will become apparent later in this chapter, there is a distinction between being in the same neighborhood and being roughly equally good; and the notion of parity illuminated by the distinction between relational judgments and categorial judgments is a version of what might be called the *same neighborhood view* (which includes cases of parity beyond cases in which the options are roughly equally good).

[4] For construals of parity in this ballpark, see Gert (2004) and Rabinowicz (2008, 2009, 2012). (Gert's construal includes an additional requirement and so is, as Rabinowicz emphasizes, more complex and demanding, but I will put aside this complication here, since it does not affect my reason for thinking that construals in this ballpark differ from the notion of parity that is at issue in this book.) See also Chang's influential discussion in *Making Comparisons Count* (2002b, chapter 5, section 5, subsection 5.3).

as, say, Chang's agent, but not on a par for another agent, say J, for whom, given his rationally permissible strong preference for the coffee over the tea, the coffee is a much better option for him than the tea. This raises the question of what positive relation holds between the coffee and the tea for an agent for whom the beverages are, in the sense that is of central concern in the current inquiry, on a par.

Here it helps to return to the distinction between categorial appraisal responses and relational appraisal responses (developed in Chapter 3), which is extremely suggestive in relation to the possibility of parity. As I will explain, in cases like Chang's coffee and tea case, the agent's assessments are best understood in terms of a combination of categorial and relational judgments, where the latter need not be based on the former.

Consider first the possibility that, in judging the tastiness of something (relative to one's own palate), one can make categorial judgments based on a considerable but not extremely large number of responses that include (appraisal) categories like the following: unspeakably horrible, terrible, really bad, bad, pretty bad, fair, fairly good, good, great, fantastic, and incredibly amazing. Consider next the possibility (explained in Chapter 3) that one can, at least in some cases, make relational judgments that are not based on first making categorial judgments and then comparing them. Given the combination of categorial and relational judgments, responses that suggest, say, one hundred comparative discriminations can (as we saw in the color case in Chapter 3) be explained with much fewer than one hundred categorial responses.

Now return to Chang's coffee or tea case and consider the judgment that the slightly more fragrant Jasmine is better than the original Jasmine. This judgment is most naturally interpreted as a relational judgment that can be arrived at without the agent first making a categorial judgment about each Jasmine and then comparing her judgments. Indeed, given the possibilities raised in the preceding paragraph, it may well be that if the agent proceeded invariably and exclusively by making a categorial judgment about each beverage—using the most refined categorial responses regarding level-of-tastiness available to her—she would put the Jasmines in the same category, say "fantastic," and so could not, via that route, arrive at the judgment that the slightly more fragrant Jasmine is better than the original Jasmine. Now consider the suggestion that the Sumatra Gold is neither better than nor worse than the Pearl Jasmine, coupled with responses to the slightly more fragrant Jasmine that speak against the suggestion that the beverages are exactly equally good, and so speak against the beverages' rankability in relation to one another. Consider, more specifically, the following four judgments:

1: The original Pearl Jasmine is not better than the Sumatra Gold.
2: The Sumatra Gold is not better than the original Pearl Jasmine.
3: The more fragrant Pearl Jasmine is better than the original Pearl Jasmine.
4: The more fragrant Pearl Jasmine is not better than the Sumatra Gold.

Here the natural interpretation of the situation is as follows: The agent's categorial response to (the tastiness of) each beverage puts the Sumatra Gold, the original Pearl Jasmine, and the more fragrant Pearl Jasmine in the same category, say "fantastic." Moreover, the agent has no relational response that grounds an intracategorial ranking of the Pearl Jasmine and the Sumatra Gold favoring one over the other. (Hence 1 and 2.) Similarly, the agent has no relational response that grounds an intracategorial ranking of the more fragrant Pearl Jasmine and the Sumatra Gold favoring one over the other. (Hence 4.) The agent does, however, have a relational response that grounds an intracategorial ranking favoring the more fragrant Pearl Jasmine over the original. (Hence 3.)

Note that my reasoning here assumes, plausibly I take it, that the presence or absence of intracategorial discriminations (concerning what matters in the choice at hand, which, in this case, is just tastiness-to-the-agent) can be relevant to judgments concerning whether, for two options in the same category, one is all-things-considered a better choice than the other (particularly, for example, when one of the options is exactly the same as the other except for one disadvantageous difference, as discussed in Chapter 3). Relatedly, insofar as intracategorial discriminations are possible, two options being in the same category does not imply that they are (exactly) equally good choices (all things considered). This leaves room for 3 (even given that the Jasmines are in the same category), which combines with 4 to yield the conclusion that the Sumatra Gold and the original Pearl Jasmine are not (exactly) equally good choices (see Chapter 1, Section 1.2). (Since 1–4 are all judgments concerning all-things-considered suitability for the purposes of choice, there is no equivocation involved in combining the claims.)

Now consider what two beverages being on a par (in terms of how they taste to you) might amount to. According to one interpretation, which I will call the broad interpretation, it amounts to the beverages being in the same category, where the relevant categories capture the *categorial* responses that carve up the *most refined* level-of-tastiness scale on which you can locate both beverages.[5] We can suppose that, in the case at hand, the set of relevant categories is {unspeakably horrible, terrible, really bad, bad, pretty bad, fair, fairly good, good, great, fantastic, incredibly amazing}, and that, for you, both the Sumatra Gold and the original Pearl Jasmine are in

---

[5] As such (and I here draw directly on a formulation suggested by Sarah Stroud in a discussion of my view), if two beverages are on a par, there is no level-of-tastiness scale of categorial responses on which you can locate both beverages such that one beverage falls squarely into one category on that scale while the other beverage falls squarely into another category on that scale. Note that I am, for the moment, abstracting from the possibility of the categories having vague boundaries. I will get to this issue shortly.

the category "fantastic." According to another interpretation, which I will call the narrow interpretation, it amounts to the beverages being in the same category (of the relevant sort) *and* there being no relational response that grounds a ranking of the beverages (in terms of how they taste to you).[6] (Note that, henceforth, I will often leave qualifications along the lines of those provided parenthetically above implicit.) According to the broad interpretation, the

---

[6] Like Nien-he Hsieh (2005), I associate parity with the possibility of options "clumping" together (as suggested by the idea of the options being "in the same league"), but my view concerning this possibility and its implications differs substantially from Hsieh's. For Hsieh, clumpiness is related to (what he sees as) the possibility of different "resolutions" correctly outputting different rankings of the same options. In Hsieh's view, two options, O1 and O2, and two resolutions, R1 and R2, can be such that A is better than B when resolution R1 is in play and A is equal (not just roughly equal) to B when resolution R2 is in play. (Hsieh illustrates his basic idea by suggesting that two student papers and two grading schemes, one more fine-grained than the other, can be such that one paper is better than the other if the more fine-grained grading scheme is in play, but the two papers are equally good if the less fine-grained grading scheme is in play.) According to Hsieh's understanding of parity and clumpiness, parity amounts to equality.

My view is closer to Yitzhak Benbaji's view, according to which parity involves "crude equality" (Benbaji 2009). But Benbaji's supporting distinction between "comprehensive degrees" of Φ-ness and "noncomprehensive degrees that scale Φ-ness" via a particular aspect of Φ-ness is, I think, not quite as relevant when it comes to assessing options for the purposes of choice. The matter is quite complicated, but, among other issues, I think that Benbaji's view obscures and distorts the possibility and significance of "all relevant aspects included" intracategorial relational judgments. Consider, for instance, an agent's correctly judging that A+ is a better choice than A when the following hold for options A, A+, and B: (1) A and B are not comparable as one better than the other or as exactly equally good but are on a par (in Benbaji's terms, they are crudely equal, rather than strictly equal or one strictly better than the other); (2) A+ and B are not comparable as one better than the other or as exactly equally good but are on a par; (3) A differs from A+ with respect to *multiple* relevant aspects, being *worse* along some, *better* along others, and slightly worse overall; and (4) the multiple aspects with respect to which A differs from A+ (say temperature and fragrance) are the same aspects with respect to which A differs from B and A+ differs from B. Suppose, for example, that A is a hot and fragrant cup of tea, A+ is a somewhat less hot but somewhat more fragrant cup of tea, and B is a tepid but extremely fragrant cup of tea, with the beverages satisfying (1)–(4) above. Then, as far as I can tell, Benbaji's position allows us to say that: (i) taking into account all relevant aspects for comparing hot beverages in terms of their tastiness to me (which include, let us assume, temperature and fragrance, perhaps among other things), A and A+ are crudely equal, in that their comprehensive degree of tastiness is "one and the same" (since comprehensive degrees of tastiness are "crude"); (ii) were all aspects but the temperature of the drinks equal, A would be better than A+; and (iii) were all aspects but the fragrance of the drinks equal, A+ would be better than A. But Benbaji's picture does not include an "all relevant aspects included" intracategorial relational judgment of A+ and A, which, in this case, is precisely what captures the superiority of A+ over A.

Sumatra Gold, the original Pearl Jasmine, and the more fragrant Jasmine are all on a par with each other. According to the narrow interpretation, the Sumatra Gold and the original Pearl Jasmine are on a par with each other, the Sumatra Gold and the more fragrant Jasmine are on a par with each other, but the original Pearl Jasmine and the more fragrant Jasmine are not on a par with each other. Both uses of "on a par" seem reasonable, and both fit with the idea that, in at least some cases of parity, the options are not comparable as one better than the other or as exactly equally good; the narrow interpretation implies that all cases of parity are such that the options are not comparable as one better than the other or as exactly equally good.

My main conclusion is that, insofar as we have both categorial responses and relational responses, with relational responses at least sometimes being direct in the sense of not being based on a comparison of categorial responses, there is nothing puzzling about so-called hard cases like the coffee or tea case in which the options are on a par and not comparable as one better than the other or as exactly equally good. Indeed, one would expect such cases to be quite common, at least when taste plays a critical role. For, if two options are in the same (appraisal) category, relational responses will often be limited to cases in which the options are quite similar to one another, as, for example, in cases where there is a small improvement along one relevant dimension, such as, for instance, fragrance. Relatedly, given very dissimilar options, relational responses will often only be available when the options are in different categories and the responses are arrived at indirectly, via comparing categorial responses to each option.

Notice that my analysis of Chang's coffee or tea case did not require an appeal to vagueness. One can add the issue of vague boundaries between categories, but the possibility of parity does not depend on this addition. The addition simply introduces a new possibility, namely the possibility of cases in which it is indeterminate whether two options are on a par.

To see this, suppose that the boundaries between (the relevant) categories are vague, and that M and N figure as "adjacent" categories. Although there can still be cases in which two options are clearly in the same category, say M, there will also be cases in which it is indeterminate whether the options are in the same category because, for one or both options, it is indeterminate whether the option qualifies as, say, M or N. According to the broad interpretation of parity articulated above, in such cases, it will be indeterminate whether the options are on a par. According to the narrow interpretation, in such cases, it may be indeterminate whether the options are on a par: more precisely, it will be indeterminate whether the options are on a par if and only if there is no relational judgment that grounds a ranking of the options. (Where there is such a judgment, the options will be determinately *not* on a par.)

4.2 Objections and Replies

In this section, I consider and respond to two possible objections to my reasoning and develop some related points.

Consider first the idea that the complication of intracategorial discriminations can be eliminated altogether by just refining categories whenever a discrimination is made. For example, "fantastic" can be subdivided into

fantastic₁ = fantastic but worse than the more fragrant Jasmine
and
fantastic₂ = not worse than the more fragrant Jasmine but not incredibly amazing,

both of which are meaningful categories (given the meaningfulness of the original categories). Notice, however, that the judgments "A is fantasic₁" and "B is fantastic₂" are, by their very construction, *hybrid* responses, each of which neatly decomposes into (1) a response that locates the object of assessment in (or else outside of) a category that captures what is, by hypothesis, a meaningful categorial judgment for the agent and (2) a relational response that compares the object of assessment to another object of assessment. The agent can use the latter response to create new groupings, but insofar as the relational response is essential to the task, the new groupings are not categories in the relevant sense—they do not capture the most refined meaningful *categorial* responses available to the agent. This takes us back to the point, emphasized by Papineau (as indicated in Chapter 3), that, insofar as we have both categorial responses and relational responses, with relational responses at least sometimes being direct in the sense of not being based on a comparison of categorial responses, it will be possible for discriminations to "outrun" categorial responses; and, when they do, we will be left with at least some intracategorial discriminations.[7]

Consider next the idea that, just because the categorial and relational responses that we have to two options do not certify them as rankable in relation to one another, it does not follow that they are not rankable in relation to one another, since our responses may fail to be sufficiently fine-tuned. This idea seems particularly plausible in light of the analogy with color perception. Notice, for instance, that nowhere does Papineau suggest that the only valid color discriminations are those that our categorial and relational responses track. Rather, Papineau suggests that, given a capacity for relational responses that do not work via a comparison of categorial responses, there is room for discriminations among colors that go beyond the discriminations that would be available via only a comparison of categorial responses. There can be color differences that we miss even when our categorial responses are supplemented with relational responses. This is, I grant, quite right. But the coffee or

---

[7] Recall that Papineau uses the term "categorical" rather than "categorial," but, as explained in Chapter 3, I've switched to the term "categorial" because it avoids some unwanted connotations when applied to appraisal responses.

tea case is particularly interesting precisely because it suggests that categorial and relational responses that speak against rankability can obtain even when it is assumed that the agent has all the information they need given what matters in the case at hand (which is what is appealing relative to the agent's subjective, sensibility-issued valuations).

Notice that the color analogy can help shed light on an interesting phenomenon associated with hard choices. Basically, the relevant empirical results are as follows: Consider four potential options A, A+, B, B+, where A+ is an improvement over A and B+ is an improvement over B. Now, focus on a case in which the choice between A+ and B+ is hard. Interestingly, the introduction of a third option sometimes makes the choice between A+ and B+ (seem) easier for the agent. When the third option is A, the agent is prone to see A+ as more appealing than B+; when the third option is B, the agent is prone to see B+ as more appealing than A+.[8] Why? Here the idea of the agent's assessment being "colored" by how the options are framed seems helpful. Recall Papineau's suggestion (discussed in Chapter 3) that, if his view concerning color perception is right, then looking at one pair of samples, say, $orange_{23}$ next to $orange_{24}$, can be just like looking at another pair of samples, say orange$_{27}$ next to $orange_{28}$. A somewhat different but related point is that if Papineau's view is right, when $orange_{23}$ is next to $orange_{24}$, looking at $orange_{23}$ can be just like looking at $peach_{14}$. Otherwise put, two colors that would, if judged singly, be categorized as orange, need not be categorized as orange when juxtaposed. Now return to the comparison between A+ and B+. Suppose that, when judged singly, A, A+, B, and B+ are all put in the same category, say "fantastic." When presented together, A+ and B+, being quite different, will naturally be compared indirectly, via a comparison of the categorial responses to each, and so will continue to be judged "fantastic." But following the introduction of, say, A, the contrast

---

[8] For a striking relevant study, see Ariely (2008, 11–15).

between A and A+ may make A+ look more categorially appealing than when it is judged singly, so that, in the context, the categorial response to A+ puts it in a "higher" category. Since A and B+ are quite different, the categorial response to B+ can plausibly be unaffected (remaining at "fantastic"). The result: A+ is now seen as more appealing than B+. This raises the question of if and when the "coloring" of the agent's categorial response to A+ by the introduction of A is to be understood as distorting. I leave this question open. In any case, when what matters is what currently appeals to the agent, A+ and B+ can count, in at least some contexts, as on a par.

4.3 Insignificant and Momentous Choices

Because my focus has been on Chang's coffee or tea case, it might seem as though the sort of parity at issue here is such that the choice between alternatives that are on a par is "insignificant": "little depends on which [option] is chosen"; "it does not matter which one chooses" (Raz 1986, 331). Joseph Raz suggests that such cases can include cases in which the options are not comparable as one better than the other or as exactly equally good. Are cases of parity, according to both the broad and narrow interpretations I have put forward, all cases in which the choice between the options is "insignificant"? Both interpretations cast parity as involving options that are in the same (appraisal) category. Can there be momentous choices between such options? Raz provides the materials for arguing that there can be. According to Raz, "what rightly makes one care about which option to choose is that each is supported by weighty, and very different reasons" (332). Relatedly, "the more comprehensive an option is, i.e. the more aspects of one's life it affects, the more important it is, other things equal" (332). Return to the case of K (in Chapter 1), who is trying to decide between career package C, in which she is a clarinetist, and career package L, in which she is a lawyer. Suppose also that this is a case in which it is permissible for K to choose on the basis of her own sensibility, but K's sensibility leaves her without a ranking of the options. Raz recognizes this as a case involving a momentous choice, and I would agree. But this is consistent with allowing that (as options for K) career package C and career package L are in the same category. Perhaps they are both fantastic. If so, then K's case counts as a case of parity according to both the broad and narrow interpretation of parity I have provided. As such, both interpretations allow for "significant" cases of parity.

4.4 Generalizing

I have been defending the idea that, insofar as we have both categorial responses and relational responses, with relational responses at least sometimes being direct in the sense of not being based on a comparison of categorial responses, there is nothing puzzling about so-called hard cases like the coffee or tea case in which the options are on a par and not comparable as one better than the other or as exactly equally good. Like the coffee or tea case, the version of K's case I considered in the preceding section is a case in which it is permissible for the agent to choose on the basis of her own sensibility. But what does parity amount to in cases in which what the agent has reason to do does not hang on the agent's sensibility? (Although some might deny that there are such cases, let us assume, for the sake of argument, that there are.) In such cases, the relevant categories need not capture the most refined categorial judgments assessing the options that are meaningful *to the agent*.

For instance, if what matters critically in a certain case is the distress caused to a patient, the relevant categories might capture the most refined level-of-distress categorial judgments that are meaningful *to the patient*. These categories might be something like the following: not distressing, ever so slightly distressing, mildly distressing, quite distressing, very distressing, extremely distressing, and excruciatingly distressing. In this case, parity can, again, be understood in terms of whether the options fall in the same category (and, if the narrow sense of parity is preferred, in terms of whether the options are comparable as one better than the other or as exactly equally good). Given the situation, the following two treatment options might figure as on a par but not comparable as one better than the other or as exactly equally good: giving the patient a series of painful shots; giving the patient a pill that will induce nausea. If A represents the first option, A– the first option plus the addition of a few more shots, and B the second option, we can have: A is not better than B, B is not better than A, A– is worse than A, and A– is not worse than B.

To take a somewhat different case, if what matters critically in the case at hand is selecting a prudent option for one's child, the relevant categories might capture the most refined categorial judgments assessing the options that are meaningful given the correct theory of prudence. These categories might be something like the following: life-shattering, extremely harmful, very harmful, quite harmful, only slightly harmful, not harmful or beneficial, mildly beneficial, quite beneficial, very beneficial, extremely beneficial, and eudaimonia-inducing. Here, the following two recreational options might figure as on a par but not comparable as one better than the other or as exactly equally good: signing Timmy up for the summer art course at the local community center or signing Timmy up for the summer soccer league at the local community center.

These are obviously toy cases, simplified to highlight a certain possibility. A lot more could be said, but I hope this suffices to suggest that there can be cases of parity even when what the agent has reason to do does not hang on the agent's sensibility. In any case, this further conclusion is not required to defend the relatively modest but highly controversial claim that at least some familiar cases that seem like cases of parity in which the options are not comparable as one better than the other or as exactly equally good, such as Chang's coffee or tea case, can be taken at face value.

4.5 Parity without Rough Equality

Significantly, my appeal to categorial appraisal responses can help explain how two options can be on a par, and so "in the same neighborhood," in terms of how valuable they are overall relative to what matters, without being roughly equally good, where to be roughly equally good, two options must be close in terms of their overall value relative to what matters in the situation, whether or not the overall value of each option can be represented as a precise point on a spectrum.

Notice first that, insofar as two options, say X and Y, are close in terms of their overall value relative to what matters in the situation, another option, say Z, that is substantially better than one of the options will be better than the other option too.[9] And then consider that, as will be illustrated presently, the "grading system" used to evaluate certain sets of options may have to employ broadly applicable evaluative terms. The result is broad evaluative classes (or leagues or neighborhoods) for which it is *not* safe to assume that all the options that are in the same evaluative class are close enough in value to count as roughly equally good; indeed, for some pairs of options in the same class, it can be clear that one of the options is much better than the other. Still, because, in accordance with the setup of the scenario provided, no more refined grading system is applicable, two options in the same evaluative class that are neither one better than the other nor exactly equally good are plausibly counted as on a par.

---

[9] See Qizilbash (2018) for related discussion concerning the "'mark of parity' on the rough equality view."

If, for instance, one is evaluating books based on whether they are worth reading, and many of the books are completely different from one another, with, for example, some having literary ambitions, others having theoretical ambitions, and others having social ambitions, dividing them up into broad (evaluative) classes, such as "poor," "fair," "good," or "exceptionally good," with intraclass rankings only for sufficiently similar options within each class, might be the only sensible way of proceeding. In particular, for some pairs of sufficiently different books, it may not be plausible to say of the books that one is better than the other or that the books are exactly equally good (in terms of being worth reading), but only that they are in the same (evaluative) class. Such books plausibly qualify as on a par (in terms of their overall value relative to what matters in the situation); but because the classes are very broad (e.g., "poor," "fair," "good," and "exceptionally good"), with substantial differences in overall value between some of the options in the same class, options in the same class cannot be assumed to be roughly equally good.

For example, two similar books in the "good" class, say A and A^ (read as "A caret"), might be such that one of the books, namely A^, is much better than the other. Of course, if all the books were very similar, one could use this information to create two new grades or sub-classes within "good," which one might label "A-level good" and "A^-level good." But insofar as some of the "good"-class books are too different to be rankable in relation to each other, this proposed grading system might not be sustainable, since if, for example, good book B cannot be ranked in relation to either A or A^, but is instead on a par with each of these books, it would have to qualify as both A-level good and A^-level good, which suggests that "A-level good" and "A^-level good" cannot be cast as distinct grade levels with A^-level good books qualifying as invariably better than A-level good books. This fits with the idea that, although options that are not rankable in relation to each other but are intuitively comparable as on a par are in the same neighborhood (in terms of how valuable they are overall relative to what matters in the situation), the relevant neighborhoods can be large, and, in particular, can include some similar options that are not roughly equally good but are instead such that one option is substantially better than the other. Relatedly, the neighborhoods can include options (like A and B) that are on a par but do not qualify as close in value because there is an option (in this case A^) that is much better than one of the options (A) but not better than the other (B). One could, of course, stipulate that all options in the same neighborhood count as roughly equally good. But this terminological move doesn't change the fact that there is a way of being close that is more demanding than being in the same neighborhood and that creates a distinct subset of cases of parity, which should be recognized as such.

Notably, the preceding discussion will, I hope, be welcomed by those who are open to the possibility of parity without rough equality but uncertain about or puzzled by Chang's controversial characterization of parity as involving a difference in value with "magnitude" but with no "bias" (in that the difference in value does not favor one of the options over the other). For, the preceding discussion suggests that we can avoid committing to Chang's characterization without accepting that all cases of parity are cases of rough equality and without losing our grip on what it is for two options that are neither one better than the other nor exactly equally good to be on a par. In particular, we can think of options that are on a par in terms of classes in a grading system that is sufficiently responsive to the complexity of the options (given what matters in the situation), without having to commit to the idea that options that are on a par have a difference in value that has magnitude but no bias. We *do* have to commit to the idea that options that are on a par fall within a(n) (evaluative) class that also includes options that are similar enough to one another to be rankable in relation to each other and whose differences in value have (nonzero) magnitude; and, for those who are receptive to Chang's characterization, the related idea that, although some pairs of options that are on a par are close in value, others are not, might be seen as fruitfully pointing to a way of understanding Chang's claim that a difference in value can have magnitude (being either small or substantial) even if it has no bias; but, for all I say above, talk of differences in value with magnitude—zero or nonzero—might, strictly speaking, only make sense in relation to options that are sufficiently similar to be rankable as one better than the other or as equally good. Notice, for instance, that, for two options X and Y that are roughly equally good but not rankable in relation to one another, what follows from the assumption that they are, in the sense described above, "close in value" relative to what matters is that an option that is much better than one of the options will be better than the other option too. This does not itself require acceptance of the claim that X and Y have a difference in value with some magnitude (even if no bias).

4.6 Conclusion

My aim in this chapter has been to illuminate the possibility of two options not being comparable as one better than the other or as exactly equally good but still being positively related to one another as "on a par." At the core of my reasoning is (a version of) the distinction between categorial responses and relational responses—a distinction that figures importantly in recent work on color perception. I suggested that parity can be helpfully understood (at least in part) in terms of categorial responses (or judgments), and showed how this leaves room for two options that are not comparable as one better than the other or as exactly equally good to be comparable as "on a par."

5

Incomparability

In Chapter 4, I supported the possibility of rationally incomplete
preferences via an appeal to incommensurable options and the related possibility of two options being neither one better than the
other nor exactly equally good but still comparable as "on a par." In
this chapter, I turn to the question of whether incommensurable
options can invariably be understood as on a par or whether some
incommensurable options are strictly incomparable. If the latter
holds, then not only is it hasty to assume that rationality requires all
options to be ranked in relation to one another, it is also hasty to assume that any two options that cannot be ranked in relation to each
other can at least be roughly compared as in the same league. The
main argument in favor of the possibility of incomparability is the
small-improvement argument, which is supposed to establish that
there are cases in which A is not better than B, and B is not better
than A, and yet A and B cannot qualify as exactly equally good because A+, which is a slightly improved version of A, is better than
A but not better than B. But, as we have seen, such cases can figure
as cases of parity, and options that are on a par are comparable as
"in the same league" and so are not completely incomparable (in
terms of how valuable they are overall relative to what matters, from
the point of view of practical reason, in the case at hand). Indeed,
since the small-improvement argument invariably involves an only
slightly improved version of one of the options, any instance of the
argument seems to support the possibility of parity rather than of
incomparability.

In light of this challenge to the small-improvement argument as
an argument for incomparability, I will propose and consider the

Choosing Well. Chrisoula Andreou, Oxford University Press. © Oxford University Press 2023.
DOI: 10.1093/oso/9780197584132.003.0006

viability of a related, seemingly more promising argument that I shall call *the huge-improvement argument for incomparability*. Ultimately, there seems to be a way around this argument too, but reflection on the argument and on getting around it is revealing. It suggests that if there are any cases of incomparability, the really interesting phenomenon in such cases is not *between* the options but *within* the options, or at least within one of them: more specifically, it suggests that cases of incomparability, if there are any, are cases in which at least one of the options is resistant to classification as positive, negative, or fairly neutral (where, by stipulation, the latter category includes, as a subset, the set of perfectly neutral options). The answer to the question of whether every (contextualized) option can be classified as positive, negative, or fairly neutral is not obvious. I will put forward a candidate case of an option that cannot be so classified, and a supporting argument, namely *the huge-improvement argument for resistance to overall evaluative classification*. This argument seems to provide a promising basis for the possibility of incomparability, but consideration of an important complication suggests that there remains a gap between the possibility of options that are resistant to classification as positive, negative, or fairly neutral, and the possibility of incomparability. In the end, what matters is that we recognize that, whether or not options can be strictly incomparable, there is room for cases beyond not just classic cases of trichotomous comparability (in which the options can be compared as either one better than the other or else as exactly equally good) but even beyond cases involving options that, although not trichotomously comparable, are still comparable as both positive, or both negative, or both fairly neutral. In the relevant further cases, at least one option is not positive, negative, neutral, or even fairly neutral. To the extent that comparability is revealed as applicable in such cases, skepticism about incomparability can persist, but its significance is reduced by the revelation of how little comparability requires.

5.1 Incomparability and the Huge-Improvement Arguments

First a quick clarificatory point about incomparability. As indicated above, incomparability is here understood as incomparability in terms of overall value relative to what matters, from the point of view of practical reason, in the case at hand. According to this philosophically familiar sense of *incomparability*, two options might count as incomparable even if one is, say, definitely better in some particular way or for some particular purpose. For example, two submissions for a creative writing contest might count as incomparable (in terms of overall value relative to what matters in the case at hand) even if one is better relative to *one* of the factors that matters given the choice situation, such as, say, originality. Similarly, the two submissions might count as incomparable in the relevant sense even if one is better in terms of a factor that is completely irrelevant given the choice situation, such as, for instance, suitability for use as a booster seat.[1]

Although any instance of the small-improvement argument seems to support the possibility of parity rather than of incomparability, it may seem an easy step from the small-improvement argument to an argument for the conclusion that some options are incomparable. All we need, it seems, is a case that satisfies the following conditions, where A↑ (read as "A upward arrow") is a huge improvement over A:

1. A is not better than B.
2. B is not better than A.

---

[1] This example is borrowed, with only slight adjustments, from Andreou (2020a). As with the attribution of similarity, the attribution of comparability is trivial apart from some specification of what matters. For an illuminating related discussion on similarity, see, for example, Goodman (1972, 437–447).

3. A↑ is better than A.

4. A↑ is not better than B.[2]

For, in such a case, one can, it seems, advance the following revisionary line of reasoning, which, supplemented with candidates for A, B, and A↑, figures as what I shall call *the huge-improvement argument for incomparability*.

> *The revisionary line of reasoning*: In cases that satisfy 1-4 (if there are any such cases), we can conclude, as in the small-improvement argument, that, not only is A not better than B and B not better than A, A and B are also not exactly equally good. But, unlike in small-improvement cases, in huge-improvement cases, there is a problem with the suggestion that it may still be true that (i) A and B are in the same league and qualify, not as incomparable, but as on a par, and (ii) the same holds for A↑ and B. The problem is that if A and B are in the same league, and A↑ is a *huge* improvement over A, it seems implausible to suggest that A↑ and B are also in the same league: A↑ must be in a higher league than B. But this conflicts with 4. It is thus more coherent to maintain that A and B are incomparable.

---

[2] The idea that a scenario involving a more-than-slightly improved option A+ might satisfy conditions 1–4 in the original small-improvement argument is suggested by Ronald de Sousa's variation on the argument, wherein the agent is supposed to be torn between "keeping her virtue" and accepting a "tempt[ing]" monetary reward for "losing it," both when the monetary reward is $1,000 and when it is substantially increased to $1,500 (de Sousa 1974). I first highlighted a huge-improvement variation of the small-improvement argument in a 2016 presentation on the topic (Tanner Humanities Center). See, relatedly, Martijn Boot's discussion of the "large improvement phenomenon" in "Problems of Incommensurability" (2017a). See also Boot's reasoning in chapter 3 of his *Incommensurability and Its Implications for Practical Reasoning, Ethics and Justice* (2017b), which includes a line of thought that is closely related to the huge-improvement argument for incomparability that I will consider presently but ultimately put aside as one that can be dismissed in something like the way the small-improvement for incomparability argument can be dismissed. A notable complication is that, for Boot, all the evaluations in play must be "detached from . . . subjective preference" (317); as such, they may fail to capture the overall evaluation of the options relative to all that matters in the case at hand from the point of view of practical reason, which can include the fit between the options and the taste or preferences of the choosing agent.

Let us see if we can supplement this argument with plausible candidates for A, B, and A↑. We can then assess the resulting huge-improvement argument for incomparability.

We can start with a variation on Joseph Raz's prominent case of an agent faced with the choice between a career as a lawyer or a career as a clarinetist (1986, 332), adding, for our current purposes, an option that is a huge improvement over one of the original options. Let A, B, and A↑ be defined as follows:

A = a career as a lawyer with compensation package M
B = a career as a clarinetist with compensation package N
A↑ = a career as a lawyer with compensation package M+H, where H is a one-time salary bonus sufficient to buy a nice home.

Suppose that, given one's sensibilities and capacities, which include musical and analytic inclinations, A is not better than B, and B is not better than A. Mightn't it also be that A↑ is better than A but not better than B? And don't we then have a case of incomparability?

One way to resist the conclusion that we have a case of incomparability is to suggest that what this case actually makes clear is that an improvement that is in some sense huge can still be *relatively* small, and so, even if A↑ is better than A but not better than B, we needn't have a case of incomparability. Instead, we can have what is, in effect, a small-improvement case in which both A and A↑ are in the same league as B. To elaborate, it might be suggested that while adding a one-time salary bonus sufficient to buy a nice home is a huge improvement to the compensation package, the addition is a relatively small improvement in relation to the career option as a whole, given the total impact on one's life of choosing a career path.[3]

---

[3] Note that the suggestion that the addition is relatively small is compatible with the idea that the relevant assessment regarding the bonus is, in Chang's terminology, relative to the "covering value" that "reflects what matters in the choice situation" and that determines how the "multiple contributory values" are to be factored into deliberation (Chang 1997). In this case, we can assume that the relevant covering value is "goodness as a career package." And we can allow that a bonus might qualify as a huge improvement

Whether or not this line of resistance is plausible in the career case, there are other cases for which it seems problematic. Suppose that one is both compassionately and philosophically inclined, and let A, B, and A↑ be defined as follows:

A = dedicating the summer to compassionately engaging with others by volunteering at a homeless shelter

B = dedicating the summer to promoting one's philosophical development by completing a book manuscript

A↑ = dedicating the summer to compassionately engaging with others by volunteering at a homeless shelter and providing a temporary foster home for a needy child.

Taking into account the context of choice, including any relevant features of the choosing agent, suppose that (from the point of view of practical reason), A is not better than B and B is not better than A. Mightn't it also be that A↑ is better than A—and, more specifically, a huge improvement over A—but not better than B? There seems to be room for this possibility, and since, in this case, the difference between A and A↑ can figure as a big part of the total impact of A↑, the improvement between A and A↑ need not qualify as relatively small.[4] Note that if it is insisted that, although they are both very substantial, volunteering at a homeless shelter for the summer is significantly "bigger" than providing a temporary foster home for a needy child, the example can be modified so that

A = dedicating the summer to compassionately engaging with others by providing a temporary foster home for a needy child.

In relation to, say, the financial dimension of a career package, without qualifying as a huge improvement in relation to the covering value "goodness as a career package."

[4] If one is inclined to think in terms of covering values, one can think of the covering value that reflects what matters in this choice situation as something like "goodness qua fruitful summer-semester project." See, relatedly, note 3 above.

Leaving B and A↑ the same as in the original example, we now have a case in which, by hypothesis, the improvement between A and A↑ is not relatively small. And there is still room for all of the following: A is not better than B, B is not better than A, A↑ is better than A, A↑ is not better than B, and A↑ is a huge improvement over A.

Suppose (returning to the original version of the summer options example) that it is granted that the improvement between A and A↑ is not relatively small and that all of the following hold: A is not better than B, B is not better than A, A↑ is better than A, A↑ is not better than B, and A↑ is a huge improvement over A. There is still room to resist the conclusion that we have a case of incomparability by suggesting that, even in this case, there is something positive we can say about how B is related to A and A↑. We can say that they are all worthwhile options (at least given the agent's interests and concerns), unlike, for example, the option of dedicating the summer to picking lint off any linty items in the area, which would presumably be a waste of time (at least for the agent in question). B thus shares an evaluative category—and so, in some sense, a league—with A and A↑: the category "worthwhile." Importantly, even though "is worthwhile" is not a binary relation, "is in the same league as" is a binary relation. And, even if we cannot make any other positive claims regarding how B compares to A and A↑ (in terms of their overall value relative to what matters, from the point of view of practical reason, in the case at hand), it seems to make sense to count A and B, as well as A↑ and B, as not simply incomparable (in terms of their overall value relative to what matters, from the point of view of practical reason, in the case at hand).

This is a viable suggestion that should, I think, be taken seriously. I will here take the suggestion on board, and grant that the huge-improvement argument for incomparability can be resisted in roughly the same way the small-improvement argument for incomparability has been resisted. Significantly, even the reader who is skeptical about the suggestion has reason to read on, since the strict construal of incomparability that goes along with taking the suggestion seriously is worth exploring even if one also allows for a less demanding construal, according to which two options can count as incomparable even if they can be related to one another as being in the same league.[5]

If the suggestion is correct, then it might seem like, even if there are slews of options that are not comparable as one better than the other or as equally good, there is no room at all for (strict) incomparability. (Henceforth, the qualifier "strict" will mostly be left implicit.) For, given a specific context of choice and a specific choosing agent, can't every option be classified as positive, negative, or fairly neutral (in terms of its overall value, given what matters, from the point of view of practical reason, in the case at hand)? If so, then one can always compare two options based on where they fall in this very rough system of classification.

The answer to the question of whether every (contextualized) option can be classified as positive, negative, or fairly neutral is not obvious. Perhaps there are options that combine positive and negative features in a way that makes it impossible to classify each option as positive (overall), negative (overall), or fairly neutral (overall). The options in the preceding candidate cases of incomparability do not seem to fit the bill; but perhaps cases involving options of the relevant sort can be found or constructed. Following, I will (1) put forward a candidate case of an option that cannot be classified as positive, negative, or fairly neutral, and (2) construct a related argument that is at the heart of what seems to be the most promising strategy for defending incomparability. I then turn to an important complication that suggests that there is a gap between the

---

[5] The seeds of the revisionary construal of incomparability that I here work out and test for applicability can be found in a couple of remarks I make in Andreou (2015b), where I briefly consider the possibility of reserving the idea of incomparability for cases in which the options cannot be compared even indirectly via a comparison of the categories they fall into in terms of their choiceworthiness.

possibility of options that are resistant to classification as positive, negative, or fairly neutral, and the possibility of incomparability; skepticism about the possibility of incomparability can thus persist. In the end, what matters is that we recognize that, whether or not options can be strictly incomparable, there is room for cases beyond not just classic cases of trichotomous comparability but even beyond cases involving options that, although not trichotomously comparable, are still comparable as both positive, or both negative, or both fairly neutral.

The idea that an option or state of affairs might not be positive, negative, or neutral (overall) is helpfully discussed by Erik Carlson (1997, 2011b), who labels states that fit this bill "indeterminate."[6] Importantly, an indeterminate state might still be categorizable as fairly neutral, in which case it will, to borrow from Nicolas Espinoza (2009), qualify as "paral," where a paral state is not exactly equally as good as a neutral state, but is on a par with a neutral state.[7] If, however, an indeterminate state is not even fairly neutral, then, even assuming that there is no ambiguity about what is or will be the case if the state obtains, it might not only fail to qualify as better than, worse than, as good as, or even roughly as good as some particular other state, it might, it seems (but more on this below), be strictly incomparable to the other state, since none of the broad category-based evaluative comparisons "both positive," "both negative," or "both fairly neutral" apply. But are there any indeterminate states of this special sort?

Consider, toward arriving at a candidate case of (strict) incomparability, the case of Abraham (or, more precisely, a stripped-down version of Abraham's case that I can extemporize as needed).

---

[6] See, relatedly, Espinoza (2009) and Gustafsson (2020).

[7] Although Carlson (2011b) allows that two options that are on a par are "comparable in an intuitive sense," given his purposes, he doesn't there distinguish between parity and incomparability, but instead stipulatively defines X and Y as incomparable if and only if it is not the case that X is at least as good as Y and it is not the case that Y is at least as good as X (57). As in Espinoza (2009), the distinction is important for my purposes here.

Abraham is ordered by God to sacrifice his son, Isaac. Suppose that, given facts about the context of choice and about Abraham's values, obeying God is, other things equal, a(n extremely) positive option, and sacrificing his son is, other things equal, a(n extremely) negative option. As John Broome describes Abraham's case, "submitting to God and saving the life of one's son are such different values that they cannot be weighed determinately against each other; that is the assumption. Neither option is better than the other, yet we also cannot say that they are equally good" (2001, 114). But this is consistent with the claim that submitting to God is positive and saving the life of one's son is positive, and so these options, although perhaps not trichotomously comparable, are not (strictly) incomparable. As such, if Abraham's case involves incomparability, we need a somewhat different, more elaborate explanation. (The same is true of similarly structured secular scenarios that involve deep but conflicting secular duties, such as patriotic versus familial duties. I use Abraham's case simply because it figures prominently in the literature on [in]comparability.)

Now consider the view that Abraham's option of obeying God and sacrificing his son is not positive (overall), negative (overall), or fairly neutral (overall). If such uncategorizability is a genuine possibility, as is suggested by initial appearances and by the argument that will be provided shortly, then perhaps Abraham's option of obeying God by sacrificing his son fails to be comparable to a variety of other options, where these other options may be positive options, negative options, fairly neutral options, or options that are not classifiable as positive, negative, or fairly neutral. Perhaps, for example, it is not comparable with the option of disobeying God by refusing to sacrifice Isaac, which may also fail to qualify as positive (overall), negative (overall), or fairly neutral (overall).

But could it really be that Abraham's option of obeying God by sacrificing his son is not positive (overall), negative (overall), or fairly neutral (overall)? Thinking inspired by the huge-improvement argument for incomparability can be helpfully imported here. In particular, we can (as part of developing what seems to be the most promising strategy for defending incomparability) construct *the huge-improvement argument for resistance to overall evaluative classification*, which—supplemented with candidates for A and A↑, where A↑ is a huge improvement over A (all things considered or given what matters in the choice situation)—can be set out as follows:

1. A is neither positive (overall) nor negative (overall).
2. A↑ is neither positive (overall) nor negative (overall).

But then:

3. A is not fairly neutral (overall), since, if it was, A↑ (which is a huge improvement over A, all things considered or given what matters in the choice situation) would be positive (overall).

So:

4. A is not positive (overall), negative (overall), or fairly neutral (overall).

Improvising a variation on Abraham's case, and taking Abraham's values (which incorporate his awe of God and his deep parental love for his son) as determining what matters in the choice situation, the following seem like plausible candidates for A and A↑:

A = obeying God by sacrificing Isaac
A↑ = obeying God and gaining an everlasting angelic proximity to God by sacrificing Isaac.

We thus have a plausible argument in favor of the possibility of an option that is not positive (overall), negative (overall), or fairly neutral (overall).

Interestingly, insofar as incomparability requires the existence of options that cannot be classified as positive, negative, or fairly neutral, the really interesting phenomenon in cases of incomparability—which I've glossed as *resistance to overall evaluative classification*—is "located" *within* the options, or at least within one of them, not *between* the options.

Note that resistance to overall evaluative classification of at least one of the options figures as a *necessary* condition for two options being incomparable; it does not figure as a *sufficient* condition. For suppose that A, A+, and A↑ are all resistant to overall evaluative classification. It can still be that each of these options is comparable to the others, with A↑ being better than A+, A+ being better than A, and A↑ being better than A. We need not, therefore, dismiss the familiar idea that incomparable options must be quite different from one another. Of course, being quite different from one another is also not a sufficient condition for two options being incomparable. The option of drinking a toxin that will make one very ill is quite different from the option of getting a relaxing massage; but one may have no difficulty at all comparing these options—the former might be obviously dismissible as terrible, and the latter appropriately embraced as great. There are thus at least two necessary conditions for two options to be incomparable: they must be quite different from one another, and at least one of the options must be resistant to overall evaluative classification. Notably, when two options are on a par, neither option can satisfy the latter condition, since, for two options to be on a par, they must be in the same league (in terms of their overall value relative to what matters, from the point of view of practical reason, in the case at hand) and so each must be categorizable (in terms of its overall value relative to what matters, from the point of view of practical reason, in the case at hand).

5.2 A Complication

I have been focusing on the question of whether there might be any incomparable options given the strict construal of incomparability according to which incomparable options not only fail to be rankable in relation to one another, but are not even comparable as in the same league. With respect to options being comparable as in the same league, I've been focusing on the ranges "positive," "negative," and "fairly neutral." Notice, however, that two options that are not comparable in relation to these ranges might be comparable given different ranges. Notice, in particular, that two options, O1 and O2, that are neither positive, nor negative, nor fairly neutral (overall) might still be such that their values are both bounded within a certain range by some positive option and some negative option.[8] For instance, if O1 combines p and n, where p is a positive feature and n is a negative feature, and O2 combines -p (i.e., not p) and -n (i.e., not n), then the value of both O1 and O2 might be bounded within the value of two options which are such that one combines p and -n and the other combines n and -p. Indeed, it might seem like the values of O1 and O2 *must* be bounded between, on the low end, an option that combines n and -p and, on the high end, an option that combines p and -n. Consider, to illustrate with a concrete example, the case of Abraham, and suppose that, because Abraham values both obeying God and not sacrificing Isaac, he considers asking God if he could sacrifice a lamb instead. That way, he could both obey God and not sacrifice Isaac (but instead a creature that is less near and dear to him); and this combination seems better than the combination of obeying God and sacrificing Isaac; similarly, it seems better than the combination of disobeying God and not sacrificing Isaac. But then the option of obeying God and sacrificing Isaac seems like it is comparable to the option of disobeying God and not sacrificing Isaac. In particular, other things

---

[8] My thanks to an anonymous journal referee for highlighting this possibility.

equal, the value of each of these options seems bounded between, on the high end, the value of obeying God and not sacrificing Isaac but a lamb instead, and, on the low end, the value of disobeying God and sacrificing Isaac rather than a lamb (where these options would become live were God to revise his order and command that a lamb be sacrificed instead of Isaac). The range picked out by these boundaries has no familiar name, but perhaps it can still be seen as a league that both purportedly incomparable options fall within (even if it lacks some of the features that characterize the leagues or categories that are of particular interest in some discussions of parity, such as the discussion in Chapter 4).

This presents an important possible complication and suggests that the idea of sharing a league might be even broader than I previously suggested. Ultimately, I'll suggest that an argument in this ballpark can be used to reintroduce skepticism about incomparability, although this will go along with the suggestion that, in some cases, saying that two options are comparable is not saying much. Notice first, however, that given the potential impact of contextual changes in value, the preceding line of thought regarding upper and lower bounds is oversimplified. Note, for instance, that, in relation to Abraham's case, it is assumed that the value of obeying God remains constant regardless of how demanding God's command is. Yet, this need not be the case. For, the positiveness of obeying God could depend on the extent to which the particular instance of obedience demonstrates a commitment to adhering to God's will whatever it is. And, if the value of obeying God's command can vary depending on how demanding it is, then we cannot assume that the value of obeying God and not sacrificing Isaac, but a lamb instead, is higher than the value of obeying God and sacrificing Isaac. Even though the latter combination is indeterminate while the former is (we can assume) positive (given Abraham's values), this is compatible with the positiveness of faithful obedience and the negativeness of personal sacrifice both being greater in the scenario requiring the greater sacrifice, and with the two possible scenarios not being rankable in relation to one another.[9] But if the value of obeying God and not sacrificing Isaac, but a lamb instead, is not higher than the value of obeying God and sacrificing Isaac, then the former cannot serve as the upper boundary of the purportedly shared league that is supposed to contain both the option of obeying God and sacrificing Isaac and the option of disobeying God and not sacrificing Isaac.

Familiarity with the original, less stripped-down version of Abraham's case might prompt the following suggestion: Consider the value of obeying God by settling on sacrificing Isaac but then not having to sacrifice Isaac because God, taking one's intention as sufficient proof of one's commitment, intervenes and retracts his command. Doesn't the value, in this scenario, of settling on sacrificing Isaac exceed the value of both of the seemingly incomparable original options (namely, obeying God and sacrificing Isaac, on the one hand, versus disobeying God and not sacrificing Isaac, on the other)? Not necessarily. For, insofar as settling on sacrificing Isaac irreparably damages Abraham's relationship to Isaac, it can fail to be better than refusing to sacrifice Isaac. But, in that case, the former option cannot serve as the upper boundary of the purportedly shared league that is supposed to contain both the option of obeying God and sacrificing Isaac and the option of disobeying God and not sacrificing Isaac.

Notice, however, that even if the option of obeying God and sacrificing Isaac and the option of disobeying God and not sacrificing Isaac are not both in a league that is bounded from *above* by some better option, they do seem (given Abraham's values) to both be in a league that is bounded from *below* by the worse option "disobeying God and sacrificing Isaac, rather than

---

[9] The possibility of a positive scenario and an indeterminate scenario not being rankable in relation to one another is emphasized in Carlson (2011b).

a lamb." Knowing that two options are in this league may not be as contentful and illuminating as knowing that two options are, say, exactly equally good (which is a case of trichotomous comparability) or that two options are, say, both fairly neutral (which is a run-of-the-mill case of parity), but it does involve knowing something (positive) about how the two options compare (rather than just knowing something about how they do *not* compare). Perhaps every pair of options can be located in a shared league with either an upper bound *or* a lower bound. If this is right, and I cannot here rule out this possibility, then, for any pair of options, the interesting question is not whether the options are comparable, but what standard(s) of comparability they meet. Are they rankable in relation to one another? Do they share a fairly narrow league or at least one that spans a qualitatively significant range (e.g., the range of positive options; or the range of negative options; or some more specific qualitatively significant range within one of these ranges, such as, say, the range of extremely negative options)? If not, then saying that they are comparable, even if true, is not saying much. (Relatedly, it is far from clear that, from the point of view of the deliberating agent, the information that two options are comparable, without further information about what standard(s) of comparability they meet, can be of much significance. By contrast, the information that, say, two options, although quite different from one another, are rankable as one better than the other might reasonably prompt the agent to seek to identify the better option. Or, the information that, say, two options, whether or not they are rankable in relation to one another, share a very narrow league might, particularly if time for deliberation is short or the cost of deliberation high, reasonably prompt the agent to just pick one of the options with the assurance that they are very close in value and so she will realize roughly the same amount of value either way.)

5.3 Conclusion

In this chapter, I focused on the question of whether all incommensurable options can be understood as on a par or whether some incommensurable options are strictly incomparable. Taking into account the serious challenge to the small-improvement argument as an argument for incomparability, I developed and assessed a variation on it that seems more promising: the huge-improvement argument for incomparability. According to my reasoning, the huge-improvement argument for incomparability is also vulnerable to a serious objection. Reflection on how one can get around the argument suggests that if there are any cases of incomparability, the really interesting phenomenon in such cases is not *between* the options but *within* the options, or at least within one of them: more specifically, it suggests that cases of incomparability, if there are any, are cases in which at least one of the options is resistant to classification as positive, negative, or fairly neutral. The answer to the question of whether every (contextualized) option can be classified as positive, negative, or fairly neutral is not obvious. I put forward a candidate case of an option that cannot be so classified, and a supporting argument, namely the huge-improvement argument for resistance to overall evaluative classification. While the argument seems to provide a promising basis for the possibility of incomparability, consideration of an important complication suggests that there remains a gap between the possibility of options that are resistant to classification as positive, negative, or fairly neutral, and the possibility of incomparability. In the end, what matters is that we recognize that, whether or not options can be strictly incomparable, there is room for cases beyond not just classic cases of trichotomous comparability but even beyond cases involving options that, although not trichotomously comparable, are still comparable as both positive, or both negative, or, even if indeterminate, both fairly neutral. In the relevant further cases, at least one option that combines a positive feature and a negative feature is not positive, negative, neutral, or even fairly neutral (overall). To the extent that comparability is revealed as applicable in such cases, skepticism about incomparability can persist, but its significance is reduced by the revelation of how little comparability requires.

6

Betterness

I have been using the distinction between categorial and relational appraisal responses to illuminate cyclic preferences and incomplete preferences, which are at least somewhat disorderly but which, in my view, can be rationally defensible. We have seen that incomplete preferences fit neatly with cases in which neither of two options is better than the other (as an option for the choosing agent), nor are the options exactly equally good. At this point, it might reasonably be wondered what connections can be drawn between rationally cyclic preferences and the relation "better than (as an option for the choosing agent)." In this chapter, I focus on the following question: If rational preferences (understood as preferences that conform to the dictates of rationality) can be cyclic, what should we conclude about the (presumed) acyclicity of the relation "better than (as an option for the choosing agent)"—where "X is better than Y (as an option for A)" is to be understood as "opting for X would be a better choice (on A's part) than opting for Y (relative to the standards of rationality, and taking into account all relevant facts, including any relevant facts about A's tastes or preferences)"? Can we hang on to the presumption that "better than (as an option for the choosing agent)" is acyclic—that, in other words, there are no betterness cycles, where a betterness cycle would involve a loop like the one in Figure 6.1?

It might seem like one must choose between the following two responses:

Response 1: "X is rationally preferred to Y (by A)" implies that X is better than Y (as an option for A); as such, rational preference

Choosing Well. Chrisoula Andreou, Oxford University Press. © Oxford University Press 2023.
DOI: 10.1093/oso/9780197584132.003.0007

Figure 6.1 Read "Y< X" as "X is better than Y."

cycles translate into betterness cycles and so undermine the presumed acyclicity of "better than."

Response 2: We cannot make sense of "better than" except insofar as we understand it as acyclic, and so we must conclude that, if A has rationally cyclic preferences, then, it must be that, for at least some X's and Y's, "X is better than Y (as an option for A)" fails to hold even though X is rationally preferred to Y (by A).

My aim is to develop an alternative response that draws on some revisionary suggestions concerning acyclicity and betterness.[1] According to the position I will develop, we should stick with the presumption that "better than" is acyclic, but my reasoning is not based on the idea that ways of understanding "better than" that allow for betterness cycles can be dismissed as not making sense. Rather, my view can be encapsulated as follows: (1) Even if there is more than one coherent way of understanding betterness, we can plausibly construe "X is better than Y (as an option for A)" as

---

[1] The crucial revisionary suggestions are described in notes 3 and 4 below.

implying that it is rationally inadvisable (for A) to choose Y from any finite set that includes both X and Y. (2) By adopting and building on this (partial) construal, we can understand betterness in a way that both preserves the acyclicity of the "better than" relation and illuminates how the divergence between "is better than" and "is rationally preferred to" is realized in cases of rationally cyclic preferences. (3) Moreover, the proposed divergence allows betterness judgments (which are supposed to concern betterness in relation to choice) to remain pertinent to choosing well in cases where following rationally cyclic preferences, although feasible given the series of choices the agent will face, will clearly lead the agent astray; and this speaks in favor of construing betterness in the way I propose.

After developing my position and replying to potential objections, I will extend my results to the relation "is morally better than" in light of the possibility that there might be moral preferability cycles.

Note that, although in my discussion of rationality and betterness, my concern will always be with whether one thing is better than another *as an option for the choosing agent*, I will often leave implicit parenthetical qualifications like "by A," "as an option for A," and "on A's part," where A is the choosing agent at issue. Note also that it will be important to keep in mind that—given that "X is better than Y (as an option for A)" is to be understood as "opting for X would be a better choice (on A's part) than opting for Y (relative to the standards of rationality, and taking into account all relevant facts, including any relevant facts about A's tastes or preferences)"— X may be better than Y as an option for A without X being better than Y in terms of promoting A's self-interest (at least if A is not rationally required to be purely self-interested). Relatedly, X may be better than Y as an option for A without it being true that X is better than Y as an option for, say, agent A* (were A* to be the choosing agent at issue).

6.1 "Is Better Than" versus "Is Rationally Preferred To"

In accordance with the standard conception of "is rationally preferred to," I will assume that X is rationally preferred to Y (by A) if and only if X is the rationally favored element of the pair (X, Y) (where A is the agent with the favoring attitude). Similarly, I will assume, as do both defenders and challengers of the possibility of rationally cyclic preferences, that showing that rational preferences can be cyclic involves identifying a set {X1, . . ., Xn} such that X2 is the rationally favored element of the pair (X1, X2), X3 is the rationally favored element of the pair (X2, X3), . . . Xn is the rationally favored element of the pair (Xn-1, Xn), but X1 is the rationally favored element of the pair (X1, Xn).[2] Although I will,

---

[2] It is worth emphasizing that, as in the case of the self-torturer, in which there is no dispute regarding the total number of distinct options that are in play, the options must not be individuated in a way that equates options that are significantly different relative to what matters. If options are improperly individuated, it may seem like the agent's preferences form a loop or cannot be understood as based on a pairwise comparison of the options, when nothing of the sort need be accepted. (For discussion of these complications in relation to versions of the fruit example that I will now present, see, for instance, Anand [1993] and, more recently, Aldred [2007]. See, relatedly, Broome [1993].)

Suppose, for example, that an agent is concerned with politeness, and that, while it is not rude to take a large fruit over a smaller fruit of a different type, it is rude to take a large fruit over a smaller fruit of the same type. Since, in this case, what matters is not just the size and type of fruit acquired via a particular selection but also whether that selection qualifies as rude, the option of, say, selecting a large apple and looking rude must not be equated with the option of selecting a large apple and not looking rude. If these options are equated, then things become muddled. Notice, for example, that if one does not flag issues of rudeness and describes options only in terms of the size and type of fruit acquired, it might seem as though the agent has the following cyclic preferences

- a large apple over a medium-sized orange,
- a medium-sized orange over a small apple, and
- a small apple over a large apple,

when the situation, more accurately described, is that the agent has the following acyclic preferences

- selecting a large apple and not looking greedy over selecting a medium-sized orange and not looking greedy,
- selecting a medium-sized orange and not looking greedy over selecting a small apple and not looking greedy, and
- selecting a small apple and not looking greedy over selecting a large apple and looking greedy.

later in the chapter, briefly consider an alternative conception of "is rationally preferred to," my goal is to show that, even if cases like the case of the self-torturer (discussed in Chapter 1) are genuine counterexamples to the acyclicity of the *standard* conception of "is rationally preferred to," we can still hang on to the presumption that "better than" is acyclic.

As indicated above, my reasoning is not based on dismissing the potential acyclicity of "better than" as incoherent.[3] Instead, it is based on the suggestion that we can—drawing on a lead that has yet to be significantly explored—plausibly construe betterness in accordance with *the inadvisability condition*.[4] According to the inadvisability

---

Similarly, if one does not flag issues of rudeness and describes options only in terms of the size and type of fruit acquired, it might seem like the agent prefers a large apple over a medium-sized orange but reverses preferences and prefers a medium-sized orange over a large apple if a small apple is added to the mix, when the situation, more accurately described, is that the agent consistently prefers selecting a large apple and not looking greedy over selecting a medium-sized orange and not looking greedy, and consistently prefers selecting a medium sized orange and not looking greedy over selecting a large apple and looking greedy. The latter description of the situation fits neatly with the idea that, when the agent's options are properly individuated, so that options that are distinct relative to what matters are not equated, it becomes clear that when a small apple is added to the mix, the crucial change is that the option of taking a large apple and not looking greedy drops out, and is replaced by the *different* option of taking a large apple and looking greedy; what varies is not the agent's preferences, but which of the agent's fixed preferences are relevant given the agent's new options.

[3] Influenced by Larry Temkin's work on transitivity and acyclicity (see, for example, Temkin 2012), I want to allow that the question of whether the "better than" of practical rationality is transitive, and so acyclic, can be plausibly understood as a substantive philosophical question, rather than as a purely terminological or logical matter. (Recall that "better than" qualifies as transitive if, for all X, Y, and Z, if X is better than Y and Y is better than Z, then X is better than Z; otherwise, the relation is intransitive. Similarly, preferences over a set of options count as transitive if the following holds: For all options X, Y, Z in the set, if X is preferred to Y and Y is preferred to Z, then X is preferred to Z; otherwise, the preferences are intransitive.)

[4] The idea of understanding "X is better than Y" in accordance with the inadvisability condition (according to which *"X is better than Y (as an option for A)" implies that it is rationally inadvisable (for A) to choose Y from any finite set (of alternatives) that includes both X and Y)* is inspired by a related proposal tentatively advanced by Arif Ahmed in some brief remarks in a comment feed concerning betterness and transitivity in *PEA Soup* (2014). Although I am not prepared to endorse Ahmed's suggestion as is, it contains an insight that I will adopt and incorporate into the supporting arguments for my position. According to Ahmed's proposal, "we can define ["Y is worse than X" or, equivalently, "X is better than Y"] to mean that [Y] is not in the favoured subset of any set to which [X and Y belong]," where favoring is a genus that includes (binary) preferring as a species. While (binary) preferring "is a function that takes every two-element option-[set] or outcome-set O to a subset of O that is in some . . . sense the 'favoured'

condition, *"X is better than Y (as an option for A)"* implies that it is *rationally inadvisable (for A) to choose Y from any finite set (of alternatives) that includes both X and Y* (where the choice of an option counts as *rationally inadvisable* if rationality advises against choosing that option, all-things considered, given the context of choice).[5,6]

subset of O," favoring is a more general function, since it can take as input an option-set or outcome-set of "arbitrary size" and output a "favoured subset." Relatedly, Ahmed suggests that, "given intransitive preferences," it doesn't follow from X being preferred to Y that, for every set containing X and Y, Y is not in the favored subset of that set. X can thus be preferred to Y without being better than Y (according to Ahmed's definition of "better than"). The relationship between Ahmed's definition and my suggestion that we understand "X is better than Y" as implying that it is rationally inadvisable to choose Y from any finite set that includes both X and Y is complicated, but at least some of my reasons for deviating from Ahmed's proposal can be captured fairly concisely. Notice, in particular, that "better than"—or at least the notion of "better than" I am concerned with in this chapter—is a normative concept, while favoring (understood as "a genus that includes (binary) preferring as a species") is a descriptive concept, and so Ahmed's definition cannot be quite right—at least not for my purposes. Also, without any constraints on favoring, "X is better than Y" cannot be transitive (as I want to allow it is) while *meaning* (as opposed to perhaps merely implying that) "Y is not in the favored subset of any set to which X and Y belong," since, without any constraints on favoring, the following combination is possible: Y is not in the favored subset of any set to which X and Y belong, and Z is not in the favored subset of any set to which Y and Z belong, but Z is in the favored subset of a set to which X and Z belong, namely {W, X, Z}. (This point is due to a helpful conversation with fellow researchers who attended my talk at the University of Saarlandes concerning a closely related view.) Finally, I worry that the idea of a favored subset might seem like a technical "black box" and needs to be worked up to in relation to the outcome sets that I am particularly interested in, such as the outcome set the self-torturer faces. But I won't delve into the reasons for my deviations here. My aim is to follow Ahmed's lead, but to begin from what I see as a more plausible and directly pertinent starting point and to construct a more substantial and compelling defense of the acyclicity of "better than." The reader will have to wait until the end of Section 6.3 to see how this pans out. Note that despite my qualms about certain aspects of Ahmed's proposal, I whole-heartedly appreciate and here adopt Ahmed's revisionary and insightful idea that, given the possibility of cyclic preferences, determining that "X is better than Y" requires attending not just to the option set {X, Y}, but to other option sets containing X and Y as well.

[5] This formulation of the inadvisability condition is influenced by conversations with Larry Temkin. Given this formulation, the inadvisability condition leaves open the possibility that there might be cases in which an agent faces an infinite set of ever-better options, and that, in such cases, the agent is not doomed to making a rationally inadvisable choice. Relatedly, the inadvisability condition allows that, when an agent faces an infinite set of ever-better options, it may not be rationally inadvisable to choose a good option, Y, from that set, even though better options, including say X, are available. (For a case in which an agent faces an infinite set of ever-better options, see, for example, Pollock 1983.)

[6] I use the term "rationally inadvisable" rather than the term "rationally impermissible" so that my contention regarding "better than" leaves room for (without committing to) a satisficing conception of rationality according to which, in some cases, rationality

Significantly, the inadvisability condition can block the path from "X is rationally preferred to Y" to "X is better than Y" only if *X can be rationally preferred to Y (by A) without it being the case that it is rationally inadvisable (for A) to choose Y from any finite set that includes both X and Y (and so without X being better than Y according to the inadvisability condition)*. If rational preferences are acyclic, then it is hard to see how this purported possibility could ever obtain. If, however, rational preferences can be cyclic (as we are here assuming), then, as will soon become apparent, its obtainability follows from a familiar and quite plausible assumption regarding rationality.

It is worth emphasizing that, while I want to resist the contention that rational preference cycles translate into betterness cycles, and the associated assumption that *"X is rationally preferred to Y (by A)"* implies that X is better than Y (as an option for A), I certainly want to allow that some cases in which X is rationally preferred to Y (by A) are good examples of cases in which X is better than Y (as an option for A), and, accordingly, good examples of cases in which it is rationally inadvisable (for A) to choose Y from any finite set (of alternatives) that includes both X and Y. Suppose, for instance, that A has the choice between playing golf (P), which they will enjoy

---

advises against but does not prohibit knowingly passing up a rationally optimal option in favor of a rationally sub-optimal option. Similarly, my use, later in the chapter, of "morally inadvisable" rather than "morally impermissible" ensures that a related contention I make regarding "morally better than" leaves room for (without committing to) a conception of morality according to which, in some cases, morality advises against but does not prohibit knowingly passing up a morally optimal option in favor of a morally sub-optimal option. I am at least somewhat attracted to this latter view, and so am somewhat invested in sticking with terminology that leaves room for it. But the complications raised in this note are tangential to the debate this chapter aims to contribute to, and I have no objection to someone putting the possibilities I've raised aside and equating inadvisability with impermissibility. Also, I will make no effort to accommodate more radical variations on the preceding conceptions of rationality and morality that endorse either of the following views: (1) rationality not only permits, but does not even advise against knowingly passing up a rationally optimal option in favor of a rationally sub-optimal option; (2) morality not only permits, but does not even advise against knowingly passing up a morally optimal option in favor of a morally sub-optimal option. Although I cannot argue against such conceptions here, I see them as implausible.

and which they can choose without any negative consequences, or undoing all the knots in a piece of string (U), which they will find boring and which has no redeeming value. Suppose further that, not surprisingly, A prefers P to U. In this case, it seems clear that P is rationally preferred to U by A. It also seems clear that P is better than U as an option for A. Accordingly, it seems clear that it is rationally inadvisable for A to choose U from any finite set (of alternatives) that includes both P and U; for rationality seems to clearly advise against choosing an activity that one will find boring and that has no redeeming value when a preferred activity that one will enjoy and that can be chosen without any negative consequences is available.

Now focus again on the inadvisability condition, according to which "X is better than Y (as an option for A)" implies that it is rationally inadvisable (for A) to choose Y from any finite set (of alternatives) that includes both X and Y. Given this condition, the threat to the presumed acyclicity of "better than" posed by the possibility of rationally cyclic preferences can be defused quite simply. We need only combine the inadvisability condition with the following familiar and quite plausible assumption regarding rationality:

> *The practicability assumption:* Rationality cannot be such that, even without having made any prior errors, one can be in a predicament wherein every option is rationally inadvisable (in that, for every available option, rationality advises against choosing that option, all things considered).[7]

---

[7] For a line of defense that can be used, with only tangential adjustments, to support the practicability assumption, see Andreou (2019c). (Relatedly, as indicated in note 6 above, tangential qualifications aside, I have no objection to the reader's equating inadvisability with impermissibility.) For some reasoning that is important in relation to my acceptance of the practicability assumption in the context of the issues raised in this book, see Section 3.3 in Chapter 3, where I argue that, insofar as an agent's preferences are rationally cyclic, it is rationally permissible for the agent to end up with an alternative that serves their preferences worse than some other alternative they could have opted for.

This assumption fits neatly with the idea that rationality cannot issue a set of demands or recommendations regarding choosing among the available alternatives that one cannot, even in principle, follow, no matter how perfectly one has been proceeding or how unambiguous and accurate one's information. In addition to being widely accepted as compelling, the assumption can be combined with the possibility of rationally cyclic preferences. It simply implies that, if an agent's preferences are rational, then, even if the preferences are cyclic, it will not be true of every available option that settling on that option is rationally inadvisable. (More on this shortly. Notably, the most controversial aspect of this implication is defended in Section 3.3 of Chapter 3, where, as just mentioned in note 7 of this section, I argue that, insofar as an agent's preferences are rationally cyclic, it is rationally permissible for the agent to end up with an alternative that serves their preferences worse than some other alternative they could have opted for.)

It follows from the inadvisability condition and the practicability assumption that "better than" is acyclic.[8] To see this, consider any finite set of alternatives S. According to the practicability assumption, there must be at least one option in the set that it is not rationally inadvisable to choose from the set. Suppose Y is such an option. Then, it follows from the inadvisability condition that, for every option X in the set, X does not qualify as better than Y; this is because X cannot count as better than Y, according to the inadvisability condition, unless it is rationally inadvisable to choose Y from any finite set containing X and Y, including S. But then the

---

I here leave open the question of whether accepting the practicability assumption involves denying the possibility of (true) rational dilemmas. For all I say here, it may be that both can be embraced via something like the following view: cases in which the options are incomparable pose rational dilemmas of a sort in that, whatever one chooses, and even if each option is eligible for rational choice, it is rationally appropriate to regret the loss of the valuable option forgone, for which the valuable option achieved is no substitute. One might embrace a parallel view regarding morally incomparable options and moral dilemmas.

[8] This passage is based on feedback from an anonymous journal referee.

options in S cannot form a betterness cycle. Since S is any finite set of alternatives, it follows that "better than" is acyclic.

Turn now to the divergence between "is better than (as an option for A)" and "is rationally preferred to (by A)" in cases involving rationally cyclic preferences. It is illuminating to see how the divergence is realized, both when there is a way of breaking the rational symmetry between the options in a preference loop, and when there is not.

Suppose an agent's preferences over the set of available alternatives are rationally cyclic. Then—as in cases in which an agent faces in *infinite* set of ever-better options—for any option Y that the agent could choose, it will be true that there is an option X that is rationally preferred to Y. Since, given the practicability assumption, rationality cannot advise against every option available to an agent who has not made any prior errors, the consideration that X is rationally preferred to Y does not, in such cases, (suffice to) make it rationally inadvisable to choose Y from the set of available alternatives. Now there are two possibilities: either there are some further features that underlie a rational asymmetry between the different options in the preference loop, or there are not.

Suppose first that there are no such further features. In particular, it is not as though the agent finds some of the options acceptable and others unacceptable. Perhaps all the options are in the same ballpark, say, "pretty good." Since, as explained in the preceding paragraph, the consideration that X is rationally preferred to Y does not make it rationally inadvisable to choose Y from the set of options in the preference loop, and since there are no further features to underlie a rational asymmetry between the options, there is nothing that would make it rationally inadvisable to choose Y from the set of options in the preference loop. So, for any option Z in the agent's preference loop, it is not the case that it is rationally inadvisable to choose Y from any finite set that includes both Z and Y. It is thus not the case that Z is better than Y. Since Y and Z can be any options in the agent's preference loop, it follows that, in this sort of case, none of the options count as better than any of the others. Suppose alternatively that there are some further features that underlie a rational asymmetry between the different options in the preference loop. Suppose, for example, that, as in the case of the self-torturer, some of the options are clearly acceptable to the agent, some are clearly unacceptable, and some fall in a gray area that is fuzzily bounded, in that there is no sharp cut-off-point between the options that are clearly acceptable and the options that are in the gray area, and there is no sharp cut-off-point between the options that are in the gray area and the options that are clearly unacceptable. Suppose further that there is no other relevant asymmetry to appeal to. Then it is plausible to reason as follows: Although the consideration that X is rationally preferred to Y does not make it rationally inadvisable to choose Y from the set of options in the preference loop, for *some* non-adjacent X's and Y's in the preference loop, there is something else that makes it rationally inadvisable to choose Y from the set of options in the preference loop, namely that Y is clearly unacceptable and X is clearly acceptable. Options that are clearly acceptable can be, and presumably are, better than options that are clearly unacceptable. In this case, we have a way of grounding a "better than" attribution that accords with the acyclicity of "better than."

Note, as an aside, that, in this case, the fuzzy boundaries that are in play allow that there will be pairs of options (V, W), including pairs of options that are adjacent to each other in the preference loop, such that, in relation to the acceptability or unacceptability of the options, which is, by hypothesis, the only thing that can be of decisive rational significance in this case, whether V is better than W is indeterminate, varying with different artificial sharpenings of the boundary between acceptable and unacceptable options. For example, in the case of the self-torturer, if setting seventy is in the fuzzily-bounded gray area between clearly acceptable and clearly unacceptable options, then whether setting seventy is better than setting seventy-one is indeterminate, with, for example, a positive verdict from the artificial sharpening that counts all and only settings seventy or under as acceptable and a negative verdict from the artificial sharpening that counts all and only settings seventy-one or under as acceptable.

6.2 League-Based Satisficing

Importantly, insofar as we recognize certain preference cycles as perfectly appropriate but require some rational asymmetry within a preference loop to ground a "better than" attribution, rational choice in situations involving preference loops will often crucially involve grouping options into leagues and then choosing an option in the highest league. This strategy qualifies as a sort of satisficing relative to one's preferences, since it involves choosing an option that is preferred relative to options in lower leagues, but it also involves choosing an option that is rationally dispreferred to another, since every option is rationally disprefered to another when preferences are rationally cyclic. This sort of satisficing can be distinguished from two philosophically familiar forms of satisficing that can also involve, at least loosely speaking, knowingly passing up an alternative that is preferred.[9]

One of the philosophically familiar forms of satisficing in question involves maximizing relative to the costs associated with searching for and inquiring into alternative options. Suppose, for example, that one is on one's way out the door to buy a $30 box

---

[9] Not all cases of satisficing involve knowingly passing up a better alternative (even loosely speaking). For example, in some cases of satisficing, one opts for the first satisfactory alternative, where this may or may not involve passing up a better alternative, since there may or may not be a better alternative available—indeed, satisficing may be appealing at least in part because finding out if a better alternative is available is too cognitively demanding. See, relatedly, Simon (1955) on satisficing and "psychological limits" (101).

of dumplings for a party tonight. One then recalls that a store other than the store one usually shops at, although one can't quite remember which other store, has the dumplings on sale for $28. Considering the costs in time and energy that it will take to find out which store has the dumplings on sale, one satisfices and accepts the "dispreferred deal," recognizing that, once the costs in time and energy of pursuing the "preferred deal" are taken into account, maximizing speaks in favor of accepting the "dispreferred deal." This form of satisficing is not at issue in the cases of cyclic preferences we've been considering, since we have allowed the cases to be ones in which the sorts of cost involved in the preceding shopping case are not in play.

The other philosophically familiar, although much more controversial, form of satisficing in question involves a willingness to pass up an option that is optimal relative to one's preferences and is readily available and to instead select an option that is merely good enough.[10] One might, for example, pass over the best dessert at the dessert table and opt for a dessert that is not as good, but that is nonetheless perfectly fine. This form of satisficing, which is often dismissed as irrational (or else as really maximizing relative to some cost that is not explicit), is also not at issue in the cases of cyclic preferences we have been considering, since these cases are such that there is no optimal option relative to one's preferences, although some of the options are in different leagues. Indeed, it is precisely because there is no optimal option relative to one's preferences that settling on an option that is not optimal relative to one's preferences but is in the highest available league is necessary.

It is worth emphasizing that while the neglected form of satisficing that is at issue in the cases of cyclic preferences we have been considering can play a crucial role in proper reasoning about

---

[10] See, relatedly, Slote (1989, chapter 1) on "satisficing moderation."

what to do, it does not figure as a form of satisficing with respect to seeking out better options over worse options. For, as we have seen, when two options in a preference loop are in the same league, and one option is dispreferred to the other, but there are no further features to underlie a rational asymmetry between the two options, neither option counts as better than the other. As such, choosing the dispreferred option does not amount to satisficing with respect to betterness.

It is also worth emphasizing that the importance of thinking in terms of leagues persists even if one is tempted to resist the possibility of rational preference cycles and maintain instead that (1) apparent rational preference cycles are purely illusory and that (2) although, in hard cases involving such apparent cycles, it is admittedly unrealistic, or perhaps even impossible to identify an optimal option (understood as one that satisfies the agent's rational preferences as well as or better than any alternative), there is some such option. Although this response presupposes, rather than supporting, the acyclicity of rational preferences, practically speaking, even if it were compelling, the need for league-based satisficing remains, since our ignorance would leave us with the same practical challenge as in a case involving a genuine rational preference cycle.

6.3 In Defense of Divergence

It might be objected that, although accepting the inadvisability condition and combining it with the practicability assumption allows us to hang on to the presumption that "better than" is acyclic (even given rationally cyclic preferences), the resulting gap between "X is rationally preferred to Y (by A)" and "X is better than Y (as an option for A)" makes the latter a poor guide to action, since X can fail to count as better than Y even if it is rationally preferred to Y, and respecting rational preferences is crucial to making good choices.[11] But this gets things all wrong. Respecting rational preferences when (one reasonably believes that) doing so will *not* prompt a series of choices that fails to do justice to betterness is perfectly appropriate. But, when preferences are rationally cyclic, acting on a series of judgments about what is rationally preferred to what (even if they correctly capture the appropriateness of a preferential attitude) can lead one, even when acceptable options are available, to an option that one, quite rationally, deems unacceptable (as illustrated in the case of the self-torturer). This is not so for acting on a series of judgments about what is better than what . (given the inadvisability condition and the practicability assumption). It is thus respecting betterness judgments that is crucial to making good choices.

Here is another issue to consider. I have suggested that we need not give up on the acyclicity of "better than," even given the possibility of rationally cyclic preferences. Based on the inadvisability condition and the practicability assumption, we can instead resist the contention that rational preference cycles translate into betterness cycles and the associated assumption, henceforth *the connecting assumption*, that "X is rationally preferred to Y (by A)" implies that X is better than Y (as an option for A). But mightn't someone favor giving up the acyclicity of "better than" over giving up the connecting assumption? If we cannot hang on to all the plausible-sounding claims that are in play in this debate, perhaps there is nothing to do but stipulate which of the claims we are going to hang on to and which we are going to give up. Or perhaps we can just distinguish between two senses of "better than"—one that sides with the connecting assumption and has no room for the acyclicity of "better than" (given the possibility of rationally cyclic preferences), and another that affirms the gap I have been positing

---

[11] This possible objection picks up on potential complications, raised in Temkin (2012), concerning the presumed significance of the "better than" relation if it is taken to be transitive (and so acyclic) even given the intransitivity of seemingly crucial associated relations.

(between "X is rationally preferred to Y [by A]" and "X is better than Y [as an option for A]") and allows for the acyclicity of "better than" (even given the possibility of rationally cyclic preferences). In the end, I can't insist on exclusive rights to the term "better than." I won't even insist that my preferred alternative is more intuitive. What I will say is that, for the reasons indicated above, it is a sense that affirms the gap I have been positing that is crucial in relation to making good choices.

Here it might be objected that, while the connecting assumption emerges as problematic in light of cases like the case of the self-torturer, my preferred alternative emerges as problematic in "one-shot" cases, wherein an agent is offered only one chance to earn $10,000 by turning on a two-setting device—call it a δ-device—that can be permanently switched from current level zero (off) to current level δ (on), where δ is the size of the tiny increment in current between adjacent settings in the case of the self-torturer.[12] Assuming that the agent reasonably values acquiring an extra $10,000, and that tiny increases in current have only the impact they are stipulated to have in the case of the self-torturer, it seems clear that switching on the δ-device is better than keeping it off. More generally, it seems clear that, in the context of a one-shot deal, "X is rationally preferred to Y" implies "X is better than Y." But this does not seem to be something my view can accommodate. Notice, for instance, that since, in the δ-device case, the agent's pre-offer pain and wealth levels are left open, the agent's experiential and financial state at current level zero can be the same as the self-torturer's experiential and financial state at some setting s where, according to my view, moving up to $s+1$, even though rationally preferred, is not better, at least not determinately better, than staying at s; and, in that case, my view seems stuck with the conclusion that switching on the δ-device is not (determinately) better than keeping it off.

---

[12] This objection is adapted from a version of the challenge raised by an anonymous journal referee.

More generally, my view seems stuck with the conclusion that, even in the context of a one-shot deal, X can be rationally preferred to Y without being better than Y; and that seems mistaken.

But let's consider the challenging case more closely. If, on the one hand, it is possible that additional "one-shot" opportunities will come along in the future—perhaps because other folks may come around with additional δ-devices (that can be implanted alongside previously implanted devices, so that several δ-level currents can flow concurrently) and offer up the same "one-shot" deal—then we should be happy to allow that, even in the context of a "one-shot" deal, X can be rationally preferred to Y without being (determinately) better than Y. For, if it is possible that additional "one-shot" opportunities will come along (and so the choice between switching on n δ-device(s) and switching on $n+1$ δ-device(s) may extend beyond $n = 0$), then the agent is still in a situation in which acting on a series of judgments of the form "X is rationally preferred to Y" can lead her, even when acceptable options are available, to an option that she, quite rationally, deems unacceptable; and this possibility problematizes the idea that, in the context of a (so-called) "one-shot" deal (that might be preceded and followed by additional "one-shot" deals), if X is rationally preferred to Y, then X is better than Y. In short, if serial "one-shot" deals are not ruled out, then we should not accept that, for "one-shot" deals, "X is rationally preferred to Y" implies "X is better than Y." Moreover, we should hold fast to the idea that betterness takes precedence over rational preferences, in that unswervingly following one's rational preferences is appropriate only when (one reasonably believes that) doing so will *not* prompt a series of choices that fails to do justice to betterness.[13]

---

[13] Notably, if, in a particular "one-shot" case of the sort under consideration, one is appropriately extremely confident that the possibility of an additional "one-shot" deal coming along will not be realized (perhaps because the chance of an additional "one-shot" deal coming along is extremely low), it might be reasonable to assume that one can act in a way that is consistent *both* with unswervingly following one's rational preferences and with avoiding series of choices that fail to do justice to betterness. In that case, it

If, on the other hand, it is not possible that additional "one-shot" opportunities will come along, say because, by hypothesis, there could not be any other δ-devices or δ-like-mechanisms (natural or human-made) in the world, then the space of possible alternatives is being restricted in a way that impacts the application of the inadvisability condition (which can be interpreted as referring to alternatives that are in the (hypothesized) space of possible alternatives). In particular, given the restriction on the space of possible alternatives, the inadvisability condition seems perfectly compatible with the position that switching on the (unique) δ-device, call it δ^*, is better than keeping it off. For, insofar as it is not possible that another one-shot opportunity will come along, there are no alternatives to switching on either *one* δ-device in all (namely δ^*) or *zero* δ-devices in all. "Options" such as "switching on n δ-devices in all," for $n>1$, are (by hypothesis) ruled out as not possible; n must equal zero or one. As such, there is only *one* set of possible alternatives that includes both the alternative "switching on *one* δ-device in all (namely δ^*)" and the alternative "switching on *zero* δ-devices in all"; the set in question contains all and only those two possible alternatives. And in relation to this singular set of possible alternatives, switching on zero δ-devices does indeed seem rationally inadvisable. There is thus room (given my position and its commitment to the inadvisability condition) for the view that, in definitively unique one-shot cases, switching on the δ-device is better than keeping it off. More generally, I can allow that, in definitively unique one-shot cases, if X is rationally preferred to Y, then X is better than Y.

Finally, it might be suggested that both the acyclicity of "better than" and the connecting assumption that I have been resisting can be salvaged, all while preserving the idea that preferences like

---

might be that choosing a course of action that is not compatible with following one's rational preferences (e.g., opting for Y even though one prefers X) qualifies as unwarranted restraint, and so the agent might be criticizable even if her choice does not involve passing up a better option.

those of the self-torturer can be, as Quinn (1993a) maintains, "perfectly . . . appropriate," in that for each pair in the cycle such that X is preferred to Y, X is the rationally favored element of the pair (X, Y) (given the agent's concerns). For suppose we grant that, (1) preferences that form a cycle can each be perfectly appropriate in this sense, and that (2) as such, "X is the rationally favored element of the pair (X, Y)" can be cyclic. We still have two options: we can stick with the standard conception of "is rationally preferred to," according to which X is rationally preferred to Y (by A) if and only if X is the rationally favored element of the pair (X, Y) (where A is the agent with the favoring attitude), and conclude that "is rationally preferred to" can be cyclic; or we can assume that, like "X is better than Y," "X is rationally preferred to Y" implies that it is rationally inadvisable to choose Y from any finite set that includes both X and Y. Why not opt for the latter, which is consistent with the acyclicity of both "better than" and "is rationally preferred to," and allow that *"X is rationally preferred to Y (by A)" implies that X is better than Y (as an option for A)*? I'm not sure about the helpfulness of this proposed move. On the one hand, it makes room for a notion of "is rationally preferred to" whose acyclicity is not threatened even if cases like the case of the self-torturer compellingly undermine the acyclicity of "is rationally preferred to" understood in accordance with the standard conception identified above. On the other hand, insofar as the move does not involve dismissing the self-torturer's preferences as confused, but, to the contrary, builds on a discussion that presumes the preferences are fitting, we still need some way of conveying the idea that the self-torturer's cyclic preferences are perfectly appropriate; we therefore need a conception like "is rationally preferred to" that is *not* acyclic, even if we are pushed to use different terminology so that "is rationally preferred to" can be aligned with "is better than." In any case, if the move is made, my main point could then be reformulated as follows: Even if cases like the case of the self-torturer compellingly undermine the acyclicity of "is rationally preferred to" given the familiar conception of "is rationally preferred to" according to which X is rationally preferred to Y (by A) if and only if X is the rationally favored element of the pair (X, Y) (where A is the agent with the favoring attitude), we can still hang on to the presumption that "better than" is acyclic. (Of course, we can also hang on to the presumption that "better than" is acyclic if we assume instead that "X is rationally preferred to Y" implies that it is rationally inadvisable to choose Y from any finite set (of alternatives) that includes both X and Y, since cases like the case of the self-torturer do not then threaten the acyclicity of "is rationally preferred to" understood in this way.) I will henceforth abstract from the complication under consideration, and use "is rationally preferred to" without explicitly including the qualification "given the familiar conception of "is rationally preferred to" according to which X is rationally preferred to Y (by A) if and only if X is the rationally favored element of the pair (X, Y) (where A is the agent with the favoring attitude)." Relatedly, in the next section, I will use "is morally preferable to" without explicitly including the qualification "given the familiar conception of 'is morally preferable to' according to which X is morally preferable to Y if and only if X is the morally favored element of the pair (X, Y)."

6.4 Morally Better Than

My focus has been on "better than" understood in terms of rationality. Notice, however, that my points about preference and betterness in the realm of rationality can also be applied to preference and betterness in the realm of morality. In particular, insofar as there is room for "is morally preferable to" to be cyclic, there is good reason to suppose that "X is morally preferable to Y" and "X is morally better than Y" can come apart, that the latter is plausibly understood as implying that it is morally inadvisable to choose Y from any finite set that includes both X and Y, and that this allows us to hang onto the presumption that "is morally better than" is acyclic. Parallel to the case of rationality, we need only combine the moral version of the inadvisability condition, according to which "X is morally better than Y" implies that it is morally inadvisable to choose Y from any finite set that includes both X and Y, with the moral version of the practicability assumption, according to which morality cannot be such that, even without having made any prior errors, one can be in a predicament wherein every option is morally inadvisable (in that, for every available option, morality advises against selecting that option, all things considered).[14] The practicability assumption fits neatly with the plausible idea that morality cannot issue a set of demands or recommendations regarding choosing among the available options that one cannot, even in principle, follow, no matter how perfectly one has been proceeding. Moreover, the assumption can be combined with the possibility of moral preferability cycles. It simply implies that even if a set of options forms a moral preferability cycle, it is not true of every available option that settling on that option is morally inadvisable. (More on this below.)

Is there room for "is morally preferable to" to be cyclic? Here again I will simply sketch out a case that seems to be one of the relevant sort. The case is Larry Temkin's (although I will use "is morally preferable to" where Temkin uses "is [morally] better than" because I want to leave open the possibility that we should understand "is [morally] better than" as acyclic even if "is morally preferable to" is not).[15] In Temkin's case, an agent, call him T, must choose between pushing a red button and pushing a blue button. If T pushes the red button, one person will "suffer intense pain for 1,000 straight days," whereas if T pushes the blue button, 1,010 people will "suffer intense pain for one day each" (2012, 82). It is, it seems, morally

---

[14] See note 7 for a point relevant to the possibility of dilemmas, including moral dilemmas.

[15] As Temkin emphasizes, his case modifies and builds on Derek Parfit's case of the "Harmless Torturers" (Parfit 1984, 80), which Parfit characterizes as derived from Jonathan Glover's case of the reformed bandits (Glover 1975, 174–175).

preferable to push the blue button. Moreover, if T is faced with a further choice in which if he presses the blue button, the same 1,010 individuals will suffer an additional day of intense pain, whereas if he presses the red button, a new individual will suffer intense pain for 1,000 straight days, it again seems morally preferable to push the blue button. Indeed, even if T has already pressed the blue button 999 times, it seems morally preferable to press it one more time, and tack on ("just") one additional day of intense suffering for each of 1,010 people, than to push the red button and cause some new person 1,000 days of intense suffering. Relatedly, if $b^\wedge w$ stands for the 1,000 button-press sequence "press blue w times and press red thereafter," then, for all n between zero and 999, $b^\wedge n+1$ seems morally preferable to $b^\wedge n$. And yet, it seems like it is morally preferable to never press the blue button (and always press the red button instead) than to press the blue button 1,000 times, since pressing the blue button 1,000 times causes 1,010 people 1,000 days of intense suffering and pressing the red button 1,000 times causes ("only") 1,000 people 1,000 days of intense suffering. We thus seem to have the moral preferability cycle in Figure 6.2.

In light of examples such as this one, Temkin (2012) is drawn toward the conclusion that "is morally better than" can be cyclic, although he is also clearly ambivalent about this result and so opts

Figure 6.2 Read "Y < X" as "X is morally preferable to Y." "$b^\wedge w$" stands for the 1,000 button-press sequence "press blue w times and press red thereafter."

for an officially agnostic stance. We can, however, essentially accept the force of Temkin's example without accepting the conclusion he himself sees as unwelcome. As indicated above, we can instead accept the moral versions of the inadvisability condition and the practicability assumption. We can thus conclude that "is morally better than" is acyclic, and so must diverge from "is morally preferable to" in cases involving moral preferability cycles.[16]

Here's a quick sketch of how the divergence between "is morally preferable to" and "is morally better than" is realized when moral preferability is cyclic: Given a moral preferability cycle, for any option Y in the cycle, it will be true that there is an option X that is morally preferable to Y. But, given that, as per the moral version of the practicability assumption, not every option is morally inadvisable, that X is morally preferable to Y cannot make it morally inadvisable to choose Y from the set of options in the cycle. And, parallel to the domain of rationality, there are two possibilities: either there are some further features that underlie a moral asymmetry between the different options in the cycle, or there are not. If there are no such further features, then, employing essentially the same reasoning employed for the domain of rationality, it can be argued that none of the options count as morally better than any of the others. Alternatively, if there are some further features that underlie a moral asymmetry between the different options in the cycle, these features can support the conclusion that some options are morally better than others, although X does not count as morally better than Y just because X is morally preferable to Y.

Let's think about this in relation to Temkin's case. Is there any asymmetry that might push us away from the conclusion that none of the options count as morally better than any of the others? Unlike in the case of the self-torturer, it seems like in Temkin's button case,

---

[16] For a defense of the acyclicity of the "better than" relation that attempts to respond to "spectrum" cases like Temkin's without granting that a moral preferability cycle is in play, see Handfield (2014). See, relatedly, Handfield and Rabinowicz (2018).

all the options in the loop are terrible. But, insofar as what matters morally in this case is not which particular individuals suffer, but how many individuals suffer and how long each suffers, there is at least one asymmetry that we can appeal to, namely that, for at least one pair of options, namely b^0 and b^{1000}, one of the options is better than the other in one respect and the same as the other in the only remaining morally relevant respect. In particular, b^0 is better than b^{1000} in terms of how many people suffer (1,000 rather than 1,010) and the same as b^{1000} in terms of how long they each suffer (1,000 days in both cases). This is not true of the other pairs in the cycle. It can thus ground a "morally better than" attribution that accords with the acyclicity of "morally better than." And note that if there are other asymmetries, they might ground additional "morally better than" attributions.

Objections that parallel the objections I considered against my position regarding "(rationally) better than" can be raised against my position regarding "morally better than." My replies are essentially the same, and they incorporate the following crucial points: When moral preferability is cyclic, acting on a series of judgments about what is morally preferable to what can lead to an option that can, and clearly should, be avoided. This is not so for acting on a series of judgments about what is morally better than what (given the moral versions of the inadvisability condition and the practicability assumption). The gap I have been positing between moral preferability judgments and moral betterness judgments thus allows moral betterness judgments (which are supposed to concern betterness in relation to choice) to remain pertinent to making morally good choices in cases where following moral preferability judgments, although feasible given the series of choices the agent will face, will clearly lead the agent astray.

Finally, parallel to the suggestion that I considered in relation to "is (rationally) better than," it might be suggested that we can, with some rethinking of "is morally preferable to" that renders the relation acyclic, salvage both the acyclicity of "is morally better than" and the assumption that *X is morally preferable to Y implies that X is morally better than Y*, all while preserving the idea that, in some cases, cyclic moral preferences are perfectly appropriate, in that for each pair in the cycle such that X is preferred to Y, X is the morally favored element of the pair (X, Y). The suggestion can be developed in essentially the same way it was developed in the case of "is rationally preferred to," and my response is essentially the same, crucially incorporating the idea that insofar as the proposed move does not involve dismissing cyclic moral preferences as confused, but, to the contrary, builds on a discussion that presumes that cyclic moral preferences are sometimes fitting, we still need some way of conveying the idea that each preference in a compelling moral preference cycle is perfectly appropriate; we therefore cannot do without a conception like "is morally preferable to" that can be cyclic, even if we are pushed to use different terminology.

6.5 Conclusion

My aim in this chapter has been to consider the implications of proposed counterexamples to the purported acyclicity of "is rationally preferred to" and "is morally preferable to" for the purported acyclicity of the "rationally better than" and "morally better than" relations. In my view, we can plausibly construe "X is better than Y" as implying that it is rationally inadvisable to choose Y from any finite set that includes both X and Y; and by adopting and building on this (partial) construal, we can understand betterness in a way that both preserves the acyclicity of the "better than" relation and illuminates how the divergence between "is better than (as an option for A)" and "is rationally preferred to (by A)" is realized in cases of rationally cyclic preferences. Similarly, we can plausibly construe "X is morally better than Y" as implying that it is morally inadvisable to choose Y from any finite set that includes both X and Y; and by adopting and building on this (partial) construal, we can understand moral betterness in a way that both preserves the acyclicity of the "morally better than" relation and illuminates how the divergence between "is morally better than" and "is morally preferable to" is realized in cases of moral preferability cycles. Moreover, understanding "is better than" and "is morally better than" in the ways I suggest does not threaten to make "better than" and "morally better than" judgments less relevant to choice than judgments about rational preference and moral preferability. To the contrary, it makes them more relevant.

7

Resolutions and Regret
upon Going Astray

I have been exploring the implications of the idea that rationality sometimes requires, not that our preferences be neat and orderly, but instead that we proceed with caution and with an awareness of larger dynamics when our preferences are disorderly. In this chapter, I explore the proper role of resolutions and regret in cases where disorderly preferences breed temptation and threaten to lead to self-defeating patterns of choice. It is now commonly recognized that, in cases involving disorderly preferences, an agent can qualify as giving in to temptation even while acting in *accordance* with her current evaluative rankings. Intrigued by this possibility, some philosophers have taken up the task of accounting for the rational failure in play in such cases. Two (potentially compatible) lines of thought have been developed. According to one line of thought, the failure at issue comes down, more or less, to deviating from a well-grounded resolution; according to the other line of thought, the failure comes down, more or less, to deviating from a prior intention without being sufficiently responsive to the prospect of future regret in which one ends up wishing one had stuck to one's prior intention. Yet, the current appeals to resolutions and regret and some of the verdicts provided face some serious challenges. Building on recent work concerning instrumental rationality, and delving into some important complications concerning human psychology, I revisit the relevant cases of temptation and analyze them in a way that puts resolutions, rational failure, and regret in their proper places. According to the position I defend, the relevant

Choosing Well. Chrisoula Andreou, Oxford University Press. © Oxford University Press 2023.
DOI: 10.1093/oso/9780197584132.003.0008

instances of giving in to temptation, *considered individually*, are not, other things equal, instances of irrationality, and the rational permissibility of giving in is not affected, except incidentally, by the agent's having formed a prior intention on the matter. Relatedly, the object of warranted dissatisfaction in situations of the relevant type is generally not a single choice but rather a pattern of choices or omissions.

7.1 Planning Agency and the No-Regret Condition

In his influential work on temptation, Michael Bratman suggests that "in being engaged in planning agency, one seems to be committed to taking seriously how one will see matters at the conclusion of one's plan, or at appropriate stages along the way, in the case of plans or policies that are ongoing" (1999, 86). This suggestion paves the way for Bratman's idea that if one forms an intention to X, but then, at the time of action, finds oneself with an evaluative ranking that favors not-X-ing, rationality can require sticking with the intention to X if one expects that one's future evaluative rankings will favor one's having stuck with the intention to X.[1] Based on this possibility, Bratman suggests that, other things equal, one should stick with a prior intention when one can see that doing so satisfies the "no-regret condition," which is when "if you stick with your prior intention, you will be glad you did" and "if you do not stick with your prior intention, you will wish you had" (79).

---

[1] Bratman's view has evolved, but the concerns I will raise about his core ideas are not affected by his later adjustments. Bratman's most significant adjustment was to rethink his rejection of the rational priority of present evaluation in Bratman 1999 and suggest (in Bratman 2014) that his core ideas concerning the significance of regret in cases of temptation can be understood as allowing for "the rational priority of present evaluation," at least when present evaluation is appropriately responsive to the "rational pressure" that anticipated future evaluative rankings sometimes exert on current evaluative rankings.

The no-regret condition is, Bratman suggests, well-suited to handle cases of temptation—at least when the agent can anticipate the fluctuations of his evaluative rankings (as, Bratman supposes, agents facing temptation often can). Consider a case of the sort I discussed in the first part of Chapter 2, wherein the agent experiences a temporary preference reversal:[2]

> Suppose that an agent resolves to eat no more than one piece of cake after dinner, knowing that having seconds will result in lethargy and a correspondingly idle evening. Suppose further that once the cake is on the table, at which point the pleasure of enjoying it and the displeasure of showing restraint are at hand, the agent's ranking of the options of having seconds versus refraining from having seconds reverses and he eagerly helps himself to a second piece, only later regretting his indulgence.

Even though the agent's having a second helping of cake fits with his current evaluative rankings, following through with his prior intention not to have seconds satisfies the no-regret condition, and so, according to Bratman, is, other things equal, the rational thing to do (or at least will be the rational thing to do once the agent's current evaluative rankings are appropriately adjusted in light of the "rational pressure" exerted by the agent's anticipated future evaluative rankings [Bratman 2014]).

The revision also helps, Bratman suggests, with a class of cases of temptation that, unlike the cake case, do not involve a reversal in evaluative rankings, but, like the cake case, are such that avoiding temptation requires overruling (or revising), rather than adhering to, a current evaluative ranking. Consider the following case, wherein the agent's preferences are stable but cyclic (and recall that, as indicated in the introduction, I'll be loosely describing

---

[2] Although, for reasons I explain in Chapter 2, I do not consider such cases full-fledged cases of self-defeating behavior, they are currently heavily focused on.

Figure 7.1 Read "Y< X" as "X is preferred to Y."

the favoring of one option in a pair as the ranking of that option over the other—even when no ranking of all the options is to be had because the agent's preferences are cyclic).[3] An agent is at a party seated in front of a family-sized bag of chips. She wants to enjoy a few chips but does not want to overindulge. Relatedly, her preferences include the preference loop in Figure 7.1.

Taking things at face value, let us assume that there really is no perfect stopping point; instead, there are, along with some fuzzily bounded gray areas, some rationally permissible stopping points and some rationally impermissible stopping points.[4] The rationally permissible stopping points involve the agent enjoying some chips but not overindulging and the rationally impermissible stopping points involve the agent overindulging. Now suppose that, knowing that no matter how many of the chips she has had she'll want one more (as having one more won't significantly affect whether or not she has overindulged), the agent resolves to stop at ten chips. In

[3] Bratman focuses on Quinn's case of the "self-torturer" (Quinn 1993a), which is structurally similar to many familiar cases of temptation, including the one on which I will focus (which is a variation of the "fun size" cakes case in Andreou [2014a]).

[4] See Chapter 1 for considerations in favor of taking cases of this sort at face value.

discussing cases with this structure, Bratman suggests that we want a view of instrumental rationality that implies that, other things equal, the agent should stick with her prior intention, and that his view of instrumental rationality issues this verdict, since, in such cases, the agent's sticking with her prior intention satisfies the no-regret condition. Bratman's reasoning, in a nutshell, is that if the agent abandons her intention, then she cannot count on the tool of planning to stop her from following her evaluative ranking of the available options at each choice point; so, it is to be expected that she will repeatedly proceed in accordance with her evaluative ranking at each choice point and end up wishing she had stuck to her plan.

But there are two complications that raise challenges for Bratman's position. The first concerns Bratman's view regarding the relevance and applicability, in cases like the chips case, of the (purported) defeasible requirement that agents stick to intentions that satisfy the no-regret condition. The second concerns Bratman's acknowledgement that regret can be "misguided" and that an agent can thus sometimes justifiability dismiss future regret as unwarranted (1999, 81).

Bratman's reasoning regarding cases like the chips case suggests that if the agent described abandons her plan, it is to be expected that she will proceed to overindulge and end up wishing she had stuck to her plan. But this is questionable. Note first that, although scenarios in which a similarly challenged agent abandons her plan and proceeds to slide all the way down a slippery slope to the dreaded outcome are familiar, so are scenarios in which a similarly challenged agent abandons her plan but still stops herself before she goes too far (i.e., while she is still well within the vaguely bounded range originally accepted as rationally permissible). As such, the agent in the chips case need not expect that if she abandons her plan, she will proceed to overindulge. There is, after all, the option and genuine possibility that, if she abandons her plan, she will—as seems rationally required, particularly if there is a defeasible requirement to avoid regret—seize one of the perfectly good upcoming opportunities to stop in good time. Furthermore, even if she does proceed to overindulge, she need not regret having deviated from her plan. She might instead regret not having stopped in the ballpark of ten chips. But, having stopped in the ballpark of ten chips is compatible with having abandoned her plan and stopped after, say, twelve chips.[5] As such, it is far from clear that, on pain of regretting deviating from her plan, the agent must stick with her intention to stop at ten chips. In short, there is no simple route from the purported (defeasible) requirement that agents stick to intentions that satisfy the no-regret condition to the purportedly desirable verdict that an agent that finds herself in a case like the chips case should stick with her prior intention.

Consider next Bratman's acknowledgement that regret can be "misguided" and so agents can sometimes justifiability dismiss future regret as unwarranted. Presumably Bratman would grant that, similarly, there is room for an agent to judge that future regret would be warranted even though she does not expect it to be forthcoming because she expects her future self to engage in spurious rationalizations. This suggests that the rational agent will need to think about whether future regret would be warranted and, if so, what exactly should be regretted. But, as will become increasingly apparent, these questions are particularly tricky in the cases of temptation at issue, and so Bratman's suggestion that agents should, other things equal, stick with intentions that satisfy the no-regret condition does not get us as far as Bratman seems to think it does.

With the idea that regret is often suspiciously missing in cases of temptation, Richard Holton (2009) focuses heavily on the possibility of (defensively) evading regret. Return to the cake case in which the agent, at the moment of action, when the temptation is experienced at full force, reverses his evaluative ranking, gives in

---

[5] I am borrowing here from a critique I provide in Andreou (2006b) concerning Bratman's treatment (in Bratman [1999]) of Quinn's puzzle of the self-torturer.

to the temptation, and only later regrets his indulgence. Holton emphasizes that regret is not always forthcoming in cases that are otherwise structurally similar to this case (2009, 100). Perhaps even more familiar than the regretful man in the cake case is the self-defensive man who continues to justify his indulgence to himself. For Holton, the problem in cases like the cake case (assuming it is a typical case of giving in to temptation) is not that the agent is setting himself up for regret—matters would be no less problematic if his ranking reversal persisted and he thus evaded regret; the problem is that, whether or not the agent ends up regretting his deviation, he should not be reconsidering his prior resolution.

Consider a modified version of the cake case in which the agent takes a second serving and feels no regret after the fact. Although the agent initially resolves not to take seconds, when the cake is on the table and the pleasure of enjoying it and the displeasure of showing restraint are at hand, the agent's ranking of the options of having seconds versus refraining from having seconds reverses and he eagerly helps himself to a second piece. Not having seconds no longer seems like the best choice, even given his anticipated lethargy. And when, as anticipated, his overeating leads to lethargy and a correspondingly idle evening, his moment-of-choice evaluative ranking persists, and he accepts this result as worth having enjoyed a second piece of cake. Now it seems reasonable to ask: Why say that the agent should not have reconsidered his prior resolution? Does it come down to something about his prior ranking? Is the prior ranking supposed to be superior or more authentic? Obviously, it cannot claim resurging endurance, since, by hypothesis, the reversed evaluative ranking is not fleeting and may persist indefinitely.

Ultimately, Holton makes it clear that he does not want to cast giving in to temptation as a matter of abandoning a defensible original ranking and acting on an objectively inferior one. Like Bratman, he is concerned with irrational succumbing, where the charge of irrationality is not supposed to challenge the agent's basic evaluations. As such, Holton focuses on a case of temptation in which it seems presumptuous to assume that the agent's reversed ranking is defective, and yet, according to Holton, other things equal, the agent is still mistaken in reconsidering his resolution. Here is the case in question:

> Homer has not been getting much exercise, and it is starting to show. He judges, and desires, that he should do something more active. He resolves to go for a daily run, starting next Saturday morning. But as his alarm goes off early on Saturday, his thoughts start to change. He is feeling particularly comfortable in bed, and the previous week had been very draining. He could start his running next weekend. And does he really want to be an early-morning runner at all?
>
> . . . Homer's judgements are not crazy. The bed is very comfortable; he has had a hard week. Indeed it is far from obvious that someone in Homer's situation should go for a run every morning; physical fitness is surely not a prerequisite of the good life.
>
> . . . [I]f it is rational for Homer to stick with his resolution, it is at least partly because he has formed it. Suppose he had decided, reasonably enough, that early-morning runs were not for him: that, all things considered, he would rather go on as before and live with the consequences. It is hard to think that such a decision would be irrational. But, relative to that decision, getting up early on Saturday morning to go for a run would look irrational. At the very least, there is no sense in which Homer would be rationally *required* to get up, in the way that he is after having made the resolution. (2009, 138–139)

In this case, it is particularly difficult to see why, other things equal, it would be irrational for Homer to reconsider his resolution.

It might be suggested that Homer should realize that, in reconsidering his resolution, he would just be rationalizing his desire to stay in bed: he would not be "coolly" thinking about what he has most reason to do; rather, motivated by his viscerally salient desire to stay in bed, he would be looking for reasons in support of this option. His judgment would thus be "skewed" and "corrupted" by the experience of temptation (Holton 2009, 145, 148). But this attribution of corruption seems too hasty: importantly, Homer would, by hypothesis, be influenced by viable points in support of the option of staying in bed—ones that, were it permissible for him to reconsider his resolution, he could rationally accept as collectively constituting sufficient reasons for him to stay in bed. As such, his "rationalization" of his desire to stay in bed would not be a *mere rationalization*, understood as a purported justification that depends on (what clear and non-deceptive thinking would dismiss as) spurious reasons or reasoning.

Perhaps there is something about resolutions in general that we can appeal to and thus show that, other things equal, resolutions should not be reconsidered. This suggestion fits well with Holton's discussion of Homer's case and with Holton's related claim that an agent can rationally form a resolution that he believes that, *were he to reconsider at the time of action*, he should rationally abandon the resolution. This claim is consistent with the possibility that the irresolute agent's irrationality lies not in a faulty revised ranking or judgment but in his reconsidering his resolution. But why think that, other things equal, resolutions should not be reconsidered? Unlike in cases involving run-of-the-mill intentions, one normally has reason, at time of action, to be suspicious of a prior resolution's adequacy relative to one's current perspective, even if nothing unanticipated has occurred in the meantime. Indeed, according to Holton, "in the standard cases of resolutions, one believes that if one were to reconsider at the time of temptation, one *would* rationally revise (more precisely: the revision would be rational from the perspective of the state of mind at the time of reconsideration)" (2009, 154). So why think that there is "a rational requirement to have a tendency not to reconsider resolutions in the face of the temptations that they were designed to overcome" (163)? Relatedly, why think that an agent can *rationally* form a resolution that he believes that, *were he to reconsider at the time of action,* he should rationally abandon the resolution.

It might be responded that it is only via the (default) habit of not reconsidering resolutions (at least when everything proceeds as expected) that one can obtain an important benefit, namely the benefit of not succumbing to anticipated temptations. But the idea that not succumbing to temptation is a *benefit* cannot come for free. If, as Holton suggests (2009, 137), typical cases of temptation share the structure of the modified cake case (in which regret is not forthcoming), then it is far from clear that an agent is benefitted by not succumbing to temptation. (Relatedly, it is far from clear that the agent is benefitted by strengthening his willpower via not succumbing to temptation so as to be better positioned to avoid succumbing to temptation in the future. Indeed, as Holton seems to recognize [2009, 145], if there is nothing wrong with succumbing to temptation, then so-called willpower amounts to obstinacy.)

Perhaps there is no need to show that the habit of not reconsidering resolutions (at least when everything proceeds as expected) is beneficial. Perhaps it is enough to show that the alternative habit of reconsidering resolutions (even when everything proceeds as expected) conflicts with the point of resolutions and is thus irrational. Consider the following reasoning:

1. The point of a resolution is to get one to non-deliberatively follow through with a planned action; it is potentially useful when one expects (or worries) that were one to consider matters at the time of action, one would not side with the action with which one currently sides.

2. Other things equal, one should not reconsider a resolution at the time of action, since this defeats the point of having formed the resolution.

3. Since resolutions should not, other things equal, be reconsidered at the time of action, an agent who tends to not reconsider

resolutions when everything proceeds as anticipated is rational and an agent who tends to reconsider resolutions even when everything proceeds as anticipated is irrational.

This reasoning does not seem to rely on the idea that, in cases of temptation where there is a preference reversal, the agent's ranking at the time of action is inferior to her prior ranking. It also does not seem to rely on future regret. Can the reasoning provide a less controversial defense of the idea that, other things equal, the agent that gives in to temptation, as in both cake cases, is being irrational? I do not think so.

Consider the idea that, other things equal, one should not reconsider a resolution at the time of action, since this defeats the point of having formed the resolution. The logic behind this idea is quite problematic. To see this, consider first the following case. Suppose A wants B to go to a yoga retreat during spring break, but A also knows that B will want to use the time to work on her dissertation. Suppose further that A goes ahead and makes all the necessary reservations. But B, finding herself inclined to work on her dissertation, insists that the reservations be cancelled. The question then arises as to whether B is being irrational. There are no critical judgments concerning the rationality or authenticity of B's inclinations; but it is proposed that B can be charged with being irrational because cancelling the reservations would defeat the purpose of A's having made them, which is for B to go to a yoga retreat during spring break. Presumably, B could rightly respond that, while it is true that B's cancelling the reservations would defeat the purpose of A's having made them, the correct conclusion to draw is not that B should not cancel the reservations, but that A should not have made them. The charge of irrationality seems particularly difficult to defend if it is granted that, were B to consider the matter carefully rather than just going along with A's plan, we can expect that rational deliberation would prompt B to side with her inclination and rank working on her dissertation above going to the yoga retreat. Similarly, the charge of irrationality seems particularly difficult to defend if it is granted that there is no reason to think that B will, after some time, come to regret having chosen to work on her dissertation during spring break. Now suppose that A and B are time-slices of the same person. Why think that the irrationality now resides with B rather than A? Shouldn't A have recognized that her plan was problematic despite being one that fit with her current ranking of the relevant options? As she anticipated, B would not be inclined to act accordingly and reflection on the matter would only reinforce this distaste; furthermore, again, it cannot just be insisted that B should non-reflectively follow along with A's plan because not doing so would interfere with the point of A's plan (which is, as is common knowledge between A and B, specifically meant to run interference with B's inclinations). It seems that we should stick with the idea that the irrationality resides with A. A should not have formed the plan. There is, it seems, no reason to hold, as Holton does, that an agent can rationally form a resolution that she believes that, were she to reconsider at the time of action, she should rationally abandon the resolution.

7.2 What's to Regret?

Where do we go from here? First, I think it is helpful to return to the question of whether, in paradigmatic cases of temptation, we can pinpoint something that the agent should regret (given her take on what matters). Consider a version of the chips case in which the agent makes no plan and, not encountering any perfect stopping point, eats chip after chip, and so overindulges. At no point does she rank eating the bag of chips above not overindulging. She simply keeps eating one more chip, with the idea that eating one more chip won't significantly affect whether or not she has overindulged. In this case, it seems that regret is warranted, since the agent fails to achieve her goal and not because achieving it was out of her control or because she came to doubt its worthiness. But what exactly should she regret? Presumably, she should regret overindulging. Where did she go wrong? Presumably, she went wrong in not making a series of choices consistent with not overindulging. She could have made such a series of choices. For instance, she could have stopped at ten chips. Can we say that she should have stopped at ten chips? That would be too strong, since, by hypothesis, there are other rationally permissible stopping points, such as, for example, stopping at twelve chips. Here, we should, I think, follow Sergio Tenenbaum's and Diana Raffman's reasoning concerning vague goals and, without assuming that there is necessarily some local error to pinpoint, stick with the claim that the agent should have made a series of choices consistent with satisfying her vague goal—in this case, the goal of not overindulging (Tenenbaum and Raffman 2012; Tenenbaum 2020).[6] Making such a series of choices requires, as Tenenbaum and Raffman explain, that the agent exercise, at one or more points, a (rational) permission to act contrary to her current evaluative ranking at that point; but there is a lot of leeway here, since there are many acceptable stopping points. Notice that there is no requirement that the agent form a plan in advance and stick to it. All that is required is that the agent exercise the relevant permissions in good time.

Indeed, it seems consistent with Tenenbaum's and Raffman's position that, other things equal, it is not irrational for an agent in the chips case to abandon a perfectly good prior plan so long as the agent exercises the rational permissions to act contrary to her current evaluative rankings in good time. For example, even if she has a plan to stop at ten chips, she cannot be charged with irrationality for abandoning her plan and stopping at twelve instead. It is, after all, realizing an acceptable pattern that matters, and the agent has

---

[6] Whether or not there is a local error to pinpoint depends on, among other things, the sense of *local* at issue, and, as I suggest in Andreou (2014b), things are complicated by the fact that what is happening *at* a certain moment can, as Michael Thompson (2008) puts it, "reach beyond" what is happening *in* that moment.

managed to do that, and not by sheer luck but by actively exercising a permission to act contrary to a current evaluative ranking in good time.

It might be objected that an agent that plans to stop at ten chips but abandons her plan and stops at twelve instead (and not just by sheer luck) is still exhibiting a rational failure, since there is some effort involved in making one's initial plan, and so it is wasteful to make the plan and then abandon it even though there is nothing wrong with the plan. There is, it might be concluded, a default presumption in favor of prior plans: we should stick with them so long as it is rationally permissible to do so.[7]

Notice first that even if there is some waste involved in the situation and the waste makes it appropriate to charge the agent with some rational failure, the correct conclusion need not be that the rational agent will, having formed a plan, stick to it. For, it might be that the rational agent will not form a plan to stop at a specific point n in such cases to begin with; they will simply stop in good time, without investing in coming up with a specific plan in advance. By hypothesis, the cases are not ones in which a specific advance intention is needed because time for deliberation will be scarce later or to gain coordination advantages that could not be achieved via the more general intention to stop in good time. As Holton suggests (2009, 152), cases with these features would include complications that are tangential relative to the task of understanding (what is distinctive about) how intentions are helpful in cases of temptation. Importantly, if the correct conclusion is that the rational agent will not invest in coming up with a specific advance intention in cases like the chips case, we are left with a position that marginalizes planning and resolutely sticking to one's plans even more than Tenenbaum's and Raffman's position.

---

[7] Bratman (2012, 2018) defends the idea that there is a default presumption in favor of prior plans, but his defense includes complications and qualifications that would make it an oversimplification to suggest that he endorses the idea "flat out." Still, I expect that (some version of) the idea will strike many as quite plausible.

It is, however, quite plausible to argue that, even if the agent already has the general plan to stop in good time and has in mind several acceptable stopping points, it can make good sense for them to invest in adopting a specific plan in advance. Empirical evidence suggests that, even in cases where advance planning is not necessitated by time constraints on deliberation or by the demands of complex coordination, agents who form specific implementation intentions in advance are more likely to realize their goals than agents with only general plans and awareness of some acceptable implementation options (Brandstätter, Lengfelder, and Gollwitzer 2001).

Here it might be suggested that this is because the agents studied are not perfectly rational. Were they perfectly rational, they would not need the crutch of an implementation intention. Let's put aside this further possible, fairly idealistic challenge to the purported make-a-plan-and-stick-to-it requirement, and accept, at least for the sake of argument, that if there is a crutch that is helpful given our limitations, then, other things equal, it is rationally permissible to use the crutch. But in taking this approach it is important to be open-minded about how the crutch might help. And I want to suggest that reflection on how the crutch might help is consistent with accepting that there need be no irrationality in the following situation: the agent forms a plan to stop at point n; they abandon their plan (even though there is nothing wrong with it); but they still stop in good time. My suggestion is based on the idea that, in at least some cases like the chips case, forming a specific plan can provide the agent with an effective anchor point, and so need not be seen as a waste even if the plan is abandoned.

Note that I am not suggesting that introducing an anchor point is the only effective and rationally permissible crutch for us in cases like the chips case, or that adopting a specific implementation intention is the only way to introduce an effective anchor point in such cases, or that rationally adopting a specific implementation intention to stop at a particular point n will invariably effectively anchor one's behavior and thus ensure that one stops in the ballpark of n. My point is that adopting the intention to stop at a particular point n in cases like the chips case can be helpful and rational (at least for agents susceptible to anchoring) even if the intention to stop at n is somewhat (but not completely) arbitrary and does not change the array of permissible and impermissible stopping points.

There are, I grant, cases in which implementation intentions help agents realize their goals by prompting agents to non-deliberatively follow through when the time for action arrives.[8] But anchoring figures as another way in which implementation intentions can be helpful—one that is particularly significant in cases where the agent knows from their prior deliberation that the plan they settled on was somewhat arbitrary and all that really matters is that they act in good time. In these cases, the agent can easily change their mind and opt for a slightly different option, without needing to engage in further deliberation about whether that option will serve their goal well. The cases are thus ones in which the agent is particularly susceptible to abandoning their plan even if they have no time for further deliberation. But, even if their plan is abandoned, it need not thereby be doomed to pointlessness.

As many of us know from experience, specific implementation intentions are often neglected in cases where just one more indulgence won't have a decisive impact. And yet we continue to form such intentions. Moreover, when they are neglected, we don't inevitably slide along the slippery slope all the way to the dreaded outcome. Instead, even when we stop later than we planned, we often (although certainly not always) stop soon enough. The following scenarios will, I assume, strike the reader as familiar: P eats a few more chips than the small bowl he planned to eat, but stops well before eating the whole family-sized bag, even though he is tempted to continue. Q surfs the internet for a few minutes longer than the thirty-minute work break he planned on, but stops

---

[8] See Brandstätter, Lengfelder, and Gollwitzer (2001).

well before surfing the day away, even though he is tempted to continue. In both cases, the agent deviates from his plan, but does not drift too far from the point he settled on. There is thus room to see his plan not as a failed attempt at self-control, but as establishing an effective anchor point. If effective, an anchor point keeps one nearby without inflexibly pinning one down. Given the possibility of implementation intentions providing effective anchor points, it is easy to see how such intentions can help agents achieve valued goals in cases like the chips case—even if the agents deviate from their intentions.[9]

In short, I want to grant that specific implementation intentions, like the intention to stop eating after ten chips, can be quite handy for dealing with temptation; indeed, given human psychology, they can help even when they are abandoned. But they need not, and in my view do not, transform a rationally acceptable stopping point into a *uniquely* rationally acceptable stopping point.

It might be objected that there is a transparency issue that stands in the way of a *rational* agent forming a plan to, say, stop at ten chips and then abandoning her plan with the recognition that, because she is susceptible to anchoring, her plan, even if abandoned can still prompt her to stop in good time. For, given that the rational agent can anticipate that a specific plan to stop at ten chips might end up serving merely as an anchor, she can really only adopt the vague plan to stop in the ballpark of ten chips. My response to this potential objection is two-fold.

First, notice that, so long as a rational agent can think it will be rationally permissible to stick with a plan to stop at ten chips, she can form the plan even if she also thinks she *might* deviate from the plan

---

[9] Of course, anchor points are not always helpful. If there is no reason to believe that a point is in the right ballpark, then anchoring one's judgments or behavior to it is, other things equal, misguided. If, for example, the result of a spin of a wheel of fortune (with marked wedges labeled from one to one hundred) anchors my judgment concerning the percentage of African countries in the United Nations, this is not a good thing; unfortunately, research suggests that we are susceptible to anchoring of this sort (Tversky and Kahneman 1974).

and that doing so would be rationally permissible. Furthermore, nothing more threatening than this latter thought seems implicit in the anticipation that a plan to stop at ten chips *might* end up serving merely as an anchor.

Second, notice that even if a rational agent who anticipates the possibility of her plan serving merely as an anchor can only really intend to stop in the ballpark of ten chips, my key points remain intact. Like the intention to stop at ten chips, the intention to stop in the ballpark of ten chips introduces an anchor point, namely ten chips, from which the agent can deviate and still achieve her goal. The intention does not transform a rationally acceptable stopping point into a *uniquely* rationally acceptable stopping point. And, insofar as it is impermissible to deviate from this intention, this will be because the intention is vague enough to allow for acceptable deviations from the anchor point.

Next, it might be objected that abandoning a prior intention when there is nothing new to take into account undermines the agent's sense of control. But this follows only if achieving one's goals (and not just by luck) requires strictly sticking to one's intentions. If it does not, and I have argued that at least sometimes it does not, then one can sometimes deviate from one's intentions without losing faith in one's self-control or in the worth of advance intentions (which can provide effective anchor points even if abandoned). Indeed, in light of my reasoning concerning anchoring intentions, it is easy to see why someone who never, ever deviated from a still defensible intention so as to pursue an alternative defensible course might be seen as somewhat compulsive.

Still, it might be maintained that it is better to be somewhat compulsive than to ever find oneself crossing the bright line bordering the slippery slope to a dreaded outcome. But this fails to recognize that, in cases of the relevant sort, the plan-selected stopping point is itself on the slope that leads to the dreaded outcome, and the question of how slippery the slope is depends on how the plan changes things. If, as I maintain, it is rationally permissible and psychologically possible to abandon the plan, then the plan does not rationally or psychologically compel the agent to stop at the (somewhat arbitrarily) selected stopping point. Instead, the plan helps by (1) controlling the agent's conduct so long as the plan remains in place and comes to mind at critical junctures, and (2) by creating an anchor point that can continue exerting influence even if the plan is abandoned. This may not seem sufficiently fancy or foolproof, but it fits with the reality of intentions—although they can help agents exercise rational permissions to act contrary to their current evaluative rankings, they do not make the complications associated with vague goals disappear.

7.3 No Regrets

My focus in the preceding section was exclusively on cases of temptation that share the structure of the chips case. But what about cases in which the agent experiences a ranking reversal at the time of action? These cases, it might be supposed, are the really hard cases, since there is no ranking that endures all along that is being thwarted. Moreover, as Holton suggests, the ranking reversal that occurs at the time of action might persist and so regret concerning the action might never be forthcoming.

The situation can, I think, be illuminated by applying one of the ideas in the preceding section to a case that is based on Holton's case of Homer, the would-be runner. The idea in question is the idea that what an agent should regret might be not a specific choice but rather the failure to realize a series of choices necessary for an ongoing goal. The case of interest is the case of someone who resolves to go for a run in the morning, but then, upon awakening to the alarm, reconsiders, and judges that the benefit of going for a run is not worth the pain and effort that would be involved in dragging himself out of bed. Let's focus on the difficult version of the case in which the agent never regrets his choice of not dragging himself out of bed that morning. There are two ways of fleshing out this case. I will consider each in turn.

In the first version, the agent not only never regrets not dragging himself out of bed that morning, but he comes to the more general conclusion that the life of an early morning runner would be hell for him, and he would rather be in poor cardiovascular condition than suffer such a grueling existence. Perhaps the agent's general conclusion is false. Perhaps he will come to enjoy running after getting over an initial hump. In that case, it is very easy to see where he is going wrong. But what if the agent's general conclusion is not based on misinformation? Perhaps he would always find early morning runs grueling. Here it is harder to charge him with irrationality for reconsidering and abandoning his prior intention. There is, however, a related version of the case wherein it is quite clear that regret is warranted (given the agent's take on what matters) and the charge of irrationality holds.

In this second version, the agent never regrets not dragging himself out of bed that morning—after all, skipping one morning run will not make or break his chances of living a long, healthy life—but he also never abandons his goal of living a long, healthy life, which is the goal that prompted his initial resolution. In this case, if he routinely fails to go running and ends up in poor cardiovascular condition, regret seems warranted—not the regret of not having gone running that particular morning, but the regret of not having made a series of choices consistent with good cardiovascular health. Clearly this version of the case is very similar to cases of temptation, like the chips case. Although the agent experiences a ranking reversal, there is, as in cases like the chips case, a stable goal that is being thwarted. As such, we can understand what is going wrong in this preference reversal case, and in cases like it, in essentially the same way we understood what was going wrong in cases like the chips case.

It might be pointed out that, although the cases I have focused on can be understood in the way I have proposed, there are also "one-shot" cases of temptation for which my reasoning will not help us get the right verdict. Suppose, for example, that A is pregnant and expects to be going into labor in the next couple of weeks. Before going into labor, A puts not getting an epidural above getting one and so intends not to get one. She knows that the pain will be excruciating and takes that into account in her evaluation. She also realizes, however, that her evaluation may change when she is in labor, even if she remains perfectly lucid and capable of clear and motivating evaluative deliberation. Suppose that, in fact, her evaluation does change. Between contractions, while she is not in excruciating pain, she reconsiders things and her evaluation reverses: she puts getting an epidural above not getting one (and her evaluation does not depend on what clear and non-deceptive thinking would dismiss as spurious reasons or reasoning). Suppose finally that she requests an epidural and gets one. If there is a rational failure here, it seems to be in the particular choice rather than in any series of choices. But the "if" here is a big "if." Whether or not A's evaluation reverses again later on (and whether or not A anticipates such a reversal), I doubt that the verdict we want in this case is that A's reconsidering and getting the epidural is (instrumentally) irrational (assuming, still, that, at the time of her getting the epidural, A does not have a higher ranked short-range or long-range goal that is being thwarted by her getting an epidural, such as, say, the goal of having the approval of her future, differently valuing self). As such, I do not think it is a problem that my reasoning does not push us to this conclusion. If such cases, or certain related cases, are cases of (instrumental) irrationality, a further story as to why will need to be provided. I have no such story and am not convinced that there is one to be had.

7.4 Conclusion

My aim in this chapter has been to improve our understanding of temptation, and of the way well-grounded resolutions and regret figure in cases of temptation. My conclusions are as follows: (1) Despite familiar claims to the contrary, in the two sorts of cases of giving in to temptation that are of interest in this chapter (wherein there seems to be cause for concern even though the agent acts in accordance with her current evaluative rankings, which reflect permissible basic evaluations), instances of giving in to temptation, *considered individually*, are not, other things equal, instances of irrationality, and the rational permissibility of giving in is not affected, except incidentally, by the agent's having formed a prior intention on the matter. (2) The object of warranted regret in situations of the type that I have focused on is generally not a choice but rather the failure to make a series of choices consistent with an ongoing goal. (3) Not all cases of choosing an option that one ranks lower than another available option are cases of *akrasia*, wherein one acts against one's better judgment; sometimes such choices amount to acting in accordance with one's judgment that one is exercising a rational permission to deviate from one's current ranking. (4) A resolution can be helpful even if it does not track or create a point that serves as a critical test of rationality or self-control; it can help by creating a psychologically salient anchor point. (5) Even when one deviates from a resolution, it can, by creating an anchor point, still help one achieve one's goals.

8

Regret in Continued Endorsement Cases

When agents realize self-defeating patterns of choice, due perhaps to being misinformed or to being insufficiently cautious given disorderly preferences, they are liable to lament some (collection) of their prior choices. In this chapter, I consider the implications of my reasoning regarding disorderly preferences for the possibility of rational regret in cases where one chooses with care and continues to endorse one's choice as rational. In such cases, regret does not involve lamenting a prior choice, but simply mourning the loss of a forgone good.

Intuitively, it might seem like, in continued endorsement cases, an agent's regret (if it is to make sense) must be tied to the idea that the forgone good is no better than the achieved good but is also not fully made up for by the achieved good because the goods are (too) different in kind. But, if the possibility of rationally cyclic preferences is taken seriously, it becomes clear that even in continued endorsement cases, mourning the loss of a forgone good need not be tied to the idea that the loss of the good is not fully made up for by the gain of a preferred or incomparable good of a different kind. Instead, it can be tied to the need to settle, via league-based satisficing, on a dispreferred alternative. Where such settling is required, regret on the part of the agent is appropriately grounded in the idea that, although his choice was defensible relative to his concerns, he deprived himself of a preferred alternative. In such cases, the agent's loss of the forgone good cannot be

Choosing Well. Chrisoula Andreou, Oxford University Press. © Oxford University Press 2023.
DOI: 10.1093/oso/9780197584132.003.0009

softened by the thought that the loss was necessary for the gain of a preferred or incomparable good of a different sort.

8.1 Regret, Monism, and Pluralism about the Good

Philosophical discussion of the possibility of rational regret in continued endorsement cases is generally framed in terms of the following question:

Q: Can regret be appropriate in continued endorsement cases—and so even apart from any supposition that one's choice was mistaken—given a monistic theory of the good?

According to monistic theories of the good, when it comes to evaluating potential actions, there is only one good-making property and so all goods are goods of the same kind. By contrast, according to pluralistic theories of the good, there is more than one good-making property, and so goods can be of different kinds, and may even be incomparable.

Q is closely related to this further question:

Q*: Can regret be appropriate in continued endorsement cases—and so even apart from any supposition that one's choice was mistaken—if it is clear in the case at issue that only one good-making property was at stake and so all the goods involved were goods of the same kind?

Although I will largely focus on Q, my response to that question, which will be affirmative, will favor an affirmative response to Q* as well, and so will be of interest even for those who find monistic theories of the good implausible but allow that there are particular cases in which only one good-making property is at stake.

Relatedly, my response will be of interest to any theorist concerned with the following question:

Q**: Must mourning the loss of a forgone good in continued endorsement cases be tied to the idea that the loss of the good is not fully made up for by the gain of a preferred or incomparable good of a different sort?

And, indeed, it is this last question, which is of interest even if one interprets all cases of regret as cases in which there is more than one good-making property at stake, that I ultimately want to address— with reasoning revealing that the answer is "no."

As seems clear from the previous chapter, there is a sort of regret according to which regretting something involves thinking or feeling that one should have chosen otherwise, and rationally regretting something involves recognizing one's prior choice as mistaken. This is *not* the sort of regret at issue in this chapter. According to the sort of regret at issue in this chapter, regretting amounts to mourning the loss of a forgone good; and, at least for the sake of argument, I will accept the philosophically common view that, given a plurality of distinct kinds of goods, there are plenty of cases of rationally regretting that do not involve the agent seeing his prior choice as mistaken.[1] (If one finds the philosophical use of "regretting" in play here unintuitive, one can replace "regretting" with "mourning the loss of a forgone good" so as to avoid terminological dispute.) Suppose, toward illustrating the philosophically common view under consideration, that parental cheerleading and professional development are two distinct kinds of goods. Then one may rationally regret missing one's child's performance even though one correctly believes that one made the right decision in taking advantage of a competing professional

---

[1] For some relevant discussion, see, for example, Williams (1973), Hurley (1989, chapter 9), Stocker (1990, chapter 8), and Dancy (1993, chapter 7).

opportunity. Although the goods at stake may be comparable, they are not "fungible."[2]

Notice that the sort of mourning I have in mind need not be deep and life-altering. Mourning the loss of a forgone good is compatible with promptly moving on with one's life—although it is also, of course, compatible with being haunted by the loss. Mourning might even be more intellectual than felt, as when one mourns the death of a stranger at a public memorial, registering the loss as regrettable, even if not personally saddening.

But can one rationally mourn the loss of a forgone good in continued endorsement cases if it is granted that there is only one good-making property and so all goods are goods of the same kind? Consider (a slightly modified version of) Martha Nussbaum's buttered bagels case (1986, 115–116), which seems like a forceful example in favor of the view that the answer is "no."[3] Suppose that one has to choose between a plate containing one buttered bagel and another plate containing two buttered bagels. The bagels are all "the same variety, equally fresh, equally hot," etc. (115). You will get twice as much pleasure eating the double serving, and all that matters is pleasure. If you rationally choose the plate with two bagels (and there are no intervening relevant changes), could you rationally regret missing out on the good you could have had had you chosen the plate with one bagel? The answer, it is widely agreed, is "no." There is nothing of value you missed out on that you could have had by opting for the plate with one bagel. You got all the pleasure you would have gotten choosing that option and then some. Of course, you might wish you had had the option of having

---

[2] Two goods are "fungible" if some amount of one figures as a "perfect substitute" for some amount of the other, in the way that, to borrow from Richard Yetter Chappell (2015, 326–327), two ten-dollar bills (typically) figure as a perfect substitute for one twenty-dollar bill.

[3] In Nussbaum's original version, the agent's "rational principle" is to "maximize her bagel eating" (1986, 115).

all three bagels; however, having three bagels was never an option and so does not figure as a forgone good.

Now consider the following more general argument against the possibility of the sort of monistic regret considered in question Q:

> Suppose that an agent rationally mourns the loss of a forgone good. There are two possibilities:
> 1: The agent sees the forgone good as preferable to the achieved good and so no longer endorses her prior choice.
> 2: The agent does not see the forgone good as preferable to the achieved good, but does not see the loss of the forgone good as fully made up for by the gain of the achieved good.
> In 2, the agent's regret presupposes a pluralistic theory of the good.
> So, in continued endorsement cases, regret for a forgone good can be rational only given a pluralistic theory of the good.

Although this argument has some intuitive appeal, existing debate regarding the internal logic of regret raises some interesting complications, particularly in relation to the idea that, in 2, the agent's regret presupposes a pluralistic theory of the good.

Consider Thomas Hurka's influential suggestion that goods with different "intrinsic properties" can be distinct "in the way that matters for rational regret" without being goods of distinct kinds, and so "monism, [like pluralism], allows for rational regret," even in cases where the agent continues to endorse her prior choice (Hurka 1996, 566). Return to Nussbaum's buttered bagel case. According to Hurka, since the bagels in Nussbaum's example all have "the same tastes, textures, and smells, only with a different causal origin," the pleasure you forgo is not "intrinsically distinct" from the one you enjoy (1986, 566). But there can be cases in which a forgone pleasure *is* intrinsically distinct from one you enjoy, even though the same good (namely, pleasure) is at stake. Suppose, for example, you must choose between a plate containing one savory bagel and a plate containing two sweet bagels, and you choose the plate containing the two sweet bagels. The forgone pleasure of the savory bagel is intrinsically distinct from the pleasure of the sweet bagels, and so Hurka's position allows that, even if you get more pleasure from eating the two sweet bagels than you would from eating the one savory bagel, there is room for rational regret. In short, even while granting that regret would not be rational in Nussbaum's buttered bagel case, Hurka resists skepticism concerning monistic regret (of the sort considered in question Q) by distinguishing between goods of distinct kinds and goods with different "intrinsic properties."

Here skeptics about monistic regret are likely to pursue one of two strategies. On the one hand, they might maintain that if pleasure really is all that matters, then there is nothing of value you missed out on that you could have had by opting for the plate with one savory bagel. You missed out on a certain experience, call it the experience of savoriness, but insofar as what matters is not savoriness itself but the accompanying or supervening pleasure, the fact that the pleasure you enjoyed was not tied to savoriness is insignificant; just as it is insignificant, in Nussbaum's original case, that the pleasure you enjoyed was not tied to the forgone bagel. On the other hand, skeptics about monistic regret might maintain that, insofar as one convincingly makes a case for the view that there is something of value you missed out on that you could have had by opting for the plate with one savory bagel, one thereby convincingly makes a case for the view that it is not just pleasure that matters, but that there are different kinds of pleasure, each with its own distinct sort of value; we are thus pushed to pluralism about the good. Michael Stocker (1990, 268) highlights these two possibilities when he says that

some may not see . . . differences [in gustatory pleasure] as allowing for rational conflict, since they do not see it as rational to be concerned about what sort of gustatory pleasure one gets.

But even if there can be rational conflict between such pleasures, what allows for the rationality of the conflict—the difference in these pleasures as pleasures—also give an evaluative pluralism of pleasure.

8.2 From Buttered Bagels to "EverBetter" Wine and Ever-So-Tempting Potato Chips

Rather than attempting to settle this dispute, which is really more about how to understand pluralism than about how to understand regret, I will focus on developing an alternative, and alternatively motivated, defense of monistic regret (with respect to a choice that is still endorsed), and on adapting this defense to address the question that I am ultimately concerned with in this chapter, namely Q**. While Hurka's defense of monistic regret is meant to undermine the view that "regret for a forgone lesser good can be rational only given a pluralistic rather than a monistic theory of the good" (1996, 555) my defense will *not* appeal to cases in which the forgone good is a *lesser* good than the achieved good; relatedly, my reasoning will not rule out the view that, insofar as regret for a forgone *lesser* good can be rational, it must be accounted for by pluralism. My aim is not to settle debate on this issue, but to complicate existing debate concerning the internal logic of regret by exploring interesting cases of an altogether different sort, namely cases in which the agent sees the forgone good as preferable to the achieved good and yet does *not* see her prior choice as mistaken and continues to endorse it. In such cases, the forgone good need not even have different intrinsic properties than the achieved good for regret to be rational; relatedly, in such cases, mourning the loss of the forgone good is tied to certain intricacies of effective holistic decision-making that cut across monism and pluralism about the good.

To begin with, I turn from buttered bagels to "EverBetter Wine." Suppose that there is an immortal agent with, as in John Pollock's example, "a bottle of EverBetter Wine which continues to get better forever. When should [she] drink it?" (Pollock 1983, 417). (Note that instead of focusing on an immortal agent with a bottle of EverBetter Wine, we could focus on a mortal agent faced with an infinite set of increasingly better wines; but I'll stick with the original, diachronic example.)

I will assume that the agent correctly sees never drinking the wine as unacceptable, perhaps because it is her only potential source of pleasure. I will also assume that, since never drinking the wine is unacceptable, and since there is no optimal drinking point, there must be one or more points in time during which drinking the wine is rationally permissible even though drinking the wine at any such point in time is not optimal.[4] This accords with the plausible assumption that rationality cannot require the impossible and so cannot, assuming the agent has not already gone astray, prohibit every option. (See, relatedly, my discussion of rational dilemmas in Chapter 3, Section 3.3, and my discussion of the practicability assumption in Chapter 6.) If one insists that every option may be rationally prohibited, read "rationally permissible" as "not rationally mistaken," where an option counts as *rationally mistaken* (given the alternatives, the choice situation, and any relevant features of the choosing agent) only if the following condition obtains: A rationally well-constituted agent (with a clear grasp of her reasons for action and no choice but to pick from among her options, even if only by default) would definitely *not* pick that option.

Now suppose that all that matters is the pleasure one will get from drinking the wine, and that the better the wine, the greater the magnitude of the pleasure one will experience. Suppose also, at least for the sake of argument, that no matter when one drinks the wine one will experience the same kind of pleasure, with all that

---

[4] For a way of understanding the optimizing conception of rationality that allows for this, see, for example, Mintoff (1997, section 4), wherein Mintoff argues that "the optimising theory does *not* imply . . . that if one knows there is a better alternative to some action, then one ought not to perform that action" (119).

varies being the magnitude of the pleasure experienced. Finally, suppose that the agent opts to drink the wine at time t, which is a rationally permissible drinking point. Is there room for the agent to mourn the loss of the (greater) pleasure that she would have experienced had she opted to drink the wine at $t+1$? I take it that the answer is clearly "yes" and that we now have a clear case of the sort needed to provide an affirmative response to our initial question Q about monistic regret. In this case, such mourning seems particularly appropriate, since one's loss, although defensible given the challenge posed by the case in relation to effective holistic decision-making, is not even softened by the gain of a preferred or incomparable good of another sort, as might have been the case were a plurality of goods involved.

It might be suggested that, although Pollock's case is theoretically interesting, since it can be used to establish the possibility of monistic regret (with respect to a choice that is still endorsed), it is irrelevant in relation to what is actually possible for mere mortals like ourselves. (This concern regarding the potential irrelevance of the case seems particularly pressing if, in addition to not needing to worry about challenges that go along with immortality, we also do not need to worry about ever having to choose from infinite sets of increasingly attractive options.) But, even if monistic regret (with respect to a choice that is still endorsed) is only possible in cases involving an infinite set of options, and all down-to-earth cases of regret are cases in which there is more than one good-making property at stake, consideration of Pollock's case paves the way to the following important result regarding more down-to-earth cases: If one allows for vague goals (which often cannot be sharpened without putting weight on artificial distinctions that distort the agent's original concerns), then, *even in cases where there is a finite set of options*, mourning the loss of a forgone good (in relation to a choice that is still endorsed) need not be tied to the idea that the loss of the good is not fully made up for by the gain of a preferred or incomparable good of a different sort; it can instead be tied to the intricacies of effective holistic decision-making and, relatedly, to the idea that, although one's choice was defensible relative to one's concerns, one deprived oneself of a preferred alternative. My ultimate question, Q^{**}, can thus be answered with a "no" without appealing to a case involving an infinite set of options.

Put yourself in the chips case from the previous chapter, which I'll elaborate on here: You have access to a family-sized bag of chips that will not be whisked away for another hour. You value both the benefits that come with eating chips (including, say, the pleasure of biting into a savory treat) and the benefits that come with not overindulging (including, say, the satisfaction of having exhibited temperance). Notice that, whether or not these goods are of distinct kinds, for any number n, such that n is greater than zero but less than the total number of chips in the bag, eating n chips from the bag seems like the same kind of good as eating $n+1$ chips from the bag; and so the choice between these two options will not be construed as a choice between goods that are significantly different in kind. Suppose, relatedly, that your goal of not overindulging is vague in the sense that there is no sharp crossover point in the process of eating chips one at a time that takes one from not overindulging to overindulging (where the fuzzily bounded range of cases that qualify as involving overindulgence, all of which you aim to avoid, can span from mild to egregious).[5] Suppose also that, as a result (and given your appetite for chips), you find that, for each n greater than or equal to zero but less than the total number of chips in the bag, you prefer eating a total of $n+1$ chips over eating a total of n chips (and this holds whether or not you

---

[5] Note that, as my parenthetical remark in the text is meant to flag, I think that overindulging can be properly understood as both vague and graded. In a *Pea Soup* post, Richard Yetter Chappell (2016) suggests that goals or ends that are described as vague are usually better understood as just graded. But, for reasons suggested by some of the responses to his post, I disagree. In any case, Chappell acknowledges the possibility of vague goals, so he need not resist the suggestion that considering the significance of vague goals in relation to the internal logic of rational regret is still very much in order.

are, at the moment, entertaining other stopping points).[6] This is because, by hypothesis, having just one more chip will be enjoyable and will not itself make the difference between overindulging and not overindulging; accordingly, eating a total of $n+1$ chips rather than a total of n chips has a determinate advantage relative to your concerns and no determinate disadvantage (which easily explains your preference for eating a total of $n+1$ chips rather than a total of n chips). Yet you also prefer having no chips at all (although you see this as a bad option) over eating all the chips in the bag (which would qualify as a clear case of overindulging, and so as a terrible option). Relative to the preferences under consideration, which are cyclic, there is no optimal stopping point, even though there is a fuzzily bounded range of good stopping points somewhere beyond the bad option of having no chips at all but before the terrible option of eating the whole bag (and so within the range of options for which it is true that *adjacent* options are not significantly different in kind). Suppose, without loss of generality, that the good stopping points are in the ballpark of a couple of handfuls of chips. And suppose, finally—and in accordance with the appearance that your vague goal of not overindulging is "rationally innocent" (to which I will also return below)[7]—that, as in the case of the EverBetter Wine, rationality requires you to settle, somewhat arbitrarily, on a good stopping point, and that, recognizing this requirement, you do so, with the result that you stop after some relatively small number of chips, say k. (Notably, this assumes that you, like the agent who drinks the wine at time t in my elaboration of Pollock's example, have enough self-control to selectively put aside some of your preferences if you think it is rational to do so.)

---

[6] In particular, knowing (for some given n and $n+1$) that there are other stopping points available does not eliminate or reverse your preference for eating a total of $n+1$ chips over eating a total of n chips, even if it complicates matters given that, as will become apparent, this preference combines with your preferences over other pairs of options in a way that can leave you stumped about where to stop.

[7] The quoted phrase is borrowed from Tenenbaum and Raffman's discussion of vague projects in "Vague Projects and the Puzzle of the Self-Torturer" (2012).

Here, as in the wine case, and despite various important structural differences, regretting the loss of the extra pleasure you would have gotten had you drawn the line one step further (at $k+1$ rather than k) makes sense given your postulated concerns and choice situation, even if you accept your prior choice as in no way mistaken and plausibly take it that you are rationally required to settle on a dispreferred alternative. By hypothesis, your choice is somewhat arbitrary, since there is no optimal stopping point—or, in the wine case, unstopping point—relative to your preferences. Losing the extra pleasure that you could have had by drawing the line one step further is avoidable and dispreferred (as is evident if, for example, you consider your twin at the next table over who, guided by the same goods, namely the pleasure of biting into a savory treat and the satisfaction of having exhibited temperance, opted to draw the line one step further and got to relish one more chip);[8] and this seems to make your regret with respect to losing the extra pleasure that you could have had by drawing the line one step further even more understandable than in cases where the loss was necessary for a preferred or incomparable good of a different sort. (Of course, desisting from eating chips at some point early on is necessary for the good of avoiding overindulging; but, since there is no sharp crossover point in the process of eating chips one at a time that takes one from not overindulging to overindulging, one's choice is never as neat as "at n chips or never" [although, eventually, it will be clearly too late for success].)

Now it might be suggested that, because vague goals like the goal of not overindulging can prompt cyclic preferences, such goals are not rationally acceptable. But this follows only if cyclic preferences are not rationally acceptable. And, as my discussions of the money-pump argument in earlier chapters suggest, there is no solid basis for this view; moreover, the fact that many vague goals, such as the

---

[8] This point about your twin captures, with only a little variation, a suggestion by Sergio Tenenbaum in his feedback to me on this chapter.

goal of not overindulging, seem "rationally innocent" speaks in favor of the acceptability of cyclic preferences.

It is worth emphasizing that, putting aside the question of whether or not vague goals that prompt cyclic preferences can be rationally acceptable, there is nothing about the internal logic of regret that precludes an agent with vague goals from experiencing the sort of regret I have been describing, and from the regret being rational in the sense of being appropriate relative to the agent's concerns. This is important, since exploring cases of regret that are rational in this sense seems sufficient for illuminating the internal logic of regret; and this is the central task that I hope to have achieved in this chapter's inquiry regarding whether mourning the loss of a forgone good, in relation to a choice that is still endorsed, must be tied to the idea that the loss of the good is not fully made up for by the gain of a preferred or incomparable good of a different sort.

Conclusion

Choice situations can be quite messy, and they can make correspondingly messy preferences appropriate. My focus in this book has been on two ways in which preferences can be disorderly and on the sorts of situations that can make such preferences appropriate, even if naively acting on them is not.

I focused first on cyclic preferences. Cyclic preferences, which can be represented as in Figure 9.1, are often generated by situations in which there is a spectrum of options, and there are multiple factors that are relevant for comparing each pair of options, but "the relative significance of factors relevant for comparing alternatives merely differing in degree . . . differ from the relative significance of those factors for comparing alternatives differing in kind" (Temkin 1996, 194). Notice, for example, that when comparing aches or pains that differ merely in degree (e.g., one mildly uncomfortable state with a barely noticeably different mildly uncomfortable state), monetary payoff may be a very significant factor in a relational appraisal of the options (given the agent's concerns), but when comparing aches or pains that differ in kind (e.g., a mildly uncomfortable state versus an excruciatingly painful state), monetary payoff may be an insignificant factor in a relational appraisal of the options (given the agent's concerns). We thus get cases like the case of the self-torturer, wherein, for any n between zero and 999, the agent prefers (all things considered) stopping at setting $n + 1$ to stopping at setting n (since setting $n + 1$ comes with a(n) (additional) large monetary reward and there is at most a barely noticeable felt difference between the two settings), but also prefers stopping at setting zero, where he feels fine, over stopping at setting

Choosing Well. Chrisoula Andreou, Oxford University Press. © Oxford University Press 2023.
DOI: 10.1093/oso/9780197584132.003.0010

Figure 9.1 Read "Y< X" as "X is preferred to Y."

1,000, where he feels excruciating pain. Similarly, and more familiarly, we end up with cases like the dreaded chips case discussed in Chapters 7 and 8.

I then turned to incomplete preferences, which are naturally generated in cases of incommensurability, wherein two options are such that, relative to what matters in the choice situation (taking into account the agent's sensibility in cases where this is relevant), neither option is better than the other (at least not determinately so) and yet the options are not exactly equally good either. The possibility of incommensurability has been supported via appeal to small-improvement scenarios in which the agent's sensibility is of decisive significance, such as Chang's coffee and tea case. Recall that, in that case, all that matters is how the beverages under consideration taste to the agent, and, given the agent's sensibility, "the cup of Sumatra Gold tastes neither better nor worse than the cup of Pearl Jasmine and . . . although a slightly more fragrant Jasmine would taste better than the original, the more fragrant Jasmine would not taste better than the cup of coffee" (2002a, 669). Given the plausible assumption that if two options are exactly equally good, then a further option that is better than one of the options will be better than the other option as well—an assumption that is not impacted by my reasoning about rationally cyclic preferences if, as argued in Chapter 6, "better than (as an option for A)" can and should be understood as acyclic even if "is rationally preferred to (by A)" is not—it follows that, in addition to not being one better than the other, the original tea and coffee are not exactly equally good either; so they are incommensurable. But then a preference gap between the options seems perfectly appropriate. Still, like an agent with cyclic preferences, an agent with incomplete preferences is susceptible to self-defeating behavior. More specifically, as explained in Chapter 1, the agent is at risk of following a series of seemingly individually permissible steps that collectively involve her incurring a gratuitous cost.

Once it is recognized that choice situations can be quite messy, and they can make correspondingly messy preferences appropriate, it should be granted that what rationality requires is not that our preferences be neatly ordered but that we proceed with caution and with a willingness to show restraint so as to avoid realizing a self-defeating pattern of choice when our preferences are disorderly. The sort of self-defeating patterns of choice that agents with cyclic and incomplete preferences must guard against is particularly interesting because it cannot be explained in terms of the self losing control over behavior. Rather, things go badly even though the self remains at the helm (and is informed about the consequences of each option). The relevant cases of informed self-defeat are thus also cases of self-governance—a combination that seems, strictly-speaking, impossible if one abstracts away from cyclic and incomplete preferences.

Properly understanding the major pitfall associated with disorderly preferences and seeing how it can be averted involves recognizing that the subjective appraisal responses to which instrumental rationality is accountable go beyond the relational appraisal responses captured by an agent's preferences (which are the only subjective appraisal responses recognized by standard conceptions of instrumental rationality); they also include categorial subjective appraisal responses. While relational subjective appraisal responses rank options in relation to one another, categorial subjective appraisal responses place options in categories, such as, for example, "great" or "terrible." Given categorial appraisal responses, there can be asymmetries in a rational preference cycle that make it irrational to end up with some alternatives (even assuming, in accordance with my discussion of rational dilemmas in Chapter 3, Section 3.3 and my discussion of the practicability assumption in Chapter 6, that not all the alternatives can be rationally inadvisable). In particular, some options may be in higher appraisal categories than others; and, at least when there is a finite set of options, rationality prohibits making a series of moves that leaves one in an unnecessarily low appraisal category (e.g., with a terrible option when great options were available). More generally, and given the notion of betterness partially sketched out in Chapter 6, rationality prohibits a series of trades between options (in a finite set) that lands one with a worse alternative over a better alternative. This includes, for example, a series of trades from A to A−, where A− is exactly the same as A except for one disadvantageous difference.

The distinction between relational appraisal responses and categorial appraisal responses also illuminates the possibility and nature of parity. Given two options in the same (appraisal) category, relational responses are often limited to cases in which the options are quite similar to one another, as, for example, in cases where there is a small improvement along one relevant dimension. As I explained, if parity is understood (at least in part) in terms of categorial responses or judgments, this leaves room for two options that are not comparable as one better than the other or as exactly equally good to be comparable as "on a par." Moreover, insofar as a case can be made for the view that two options can always be compared as either in different "leagues," one of which is superior to the other, or else as sharing a "league," where the shared league can be very broad, options may never be strictly incomparable.

The revisionary way of understanding instrumental rationality that is suggested by the distinction between categorial and relational appraisal responses, and their connection to rationally cyclic preferences, raises major complications in relation to the presumed acyclicity of the "better than" relation. Nonetheless, the acyclicity of the "better than" relation can be maintained via combining the inadvisability condition—according to which "X is better than Y (as an option for A)" implies that it is rationally inadvisable (for A) to choose Y from any finite set (of alternatives) that includes both X and Y—and the practicability assumption—according to which rationality cannot be such that, even without having made any prior errors, one can be in a predicament wherein every option is rationally inadvisable. Happily, this preserves a construal of "better than" that fits with the idea that respecting betterness judgments is crucial to making good choices.

Notably, although we can hang on to the acyclicity of the "better than" relation, given the possibility of rationally cyclic preferences, thinking in terms of appraisal categories or leagues continues to be crucial, since rational choice will still sometimes involve league-based satisficing relative to one's preferences, wherein one chooses an option that is in the highest available league but is dispreferred relative to some other available option. Interestingly, the importance of thinking in terms of leagues persists even if one refuses to recognize the possibility of rationally cyclic preferences and maintains instead that (1) seemingly rational preference cycles are purely illusory and that (2) although, in some hard cases, it is admittedly unrealistic, or perhaps even impossible to identify an option that is optimal relative to the agent's concerns, there is invariably some such option. Although this response presupposes, rather than supporting, the acyclicity of rational preferences, practically speaking, even if it were compelling, the need for league-based satisficing remains, since our ignorance would leave us with the same practical challenge as in cases involving genuine rational preference cycles.

A failure to engage in league-based satisficing can result in cases in which the agent qualifies as giving in to temptation even though she acts in accordance with her rational preferences at each choice point. Recall the case of the agent who eats chip after chip, ultimately polishing off a family-sized bag. Given that she does not want to overindulge, she qualifies as giving into temptation, even though, at each choice point, she correctly assumes that having one more chip won't significantly affect whether or not she has overindulged. According to some philosophers, the relevant cases of temptation suggest that rationality requires that an agent come up with a plan and then resolutely stick to it; other things equal, deviating from the plan qualifies as a rational failure. By contrast, according to the position I develop in Chapter 7, the relevant instances of giving in to temptation, *considered individually*, are not, other things equal, instances of irrationality, and the rational permissibility of giving in is not affected, except incidentally, by the agent's having formed a prior intention on the matter. Relatedly, the object of warranted dissatisfaction in situations of the relevant type is generally not a single choice but rather a pattern of choices or omissions.

Interestingly, it is when an agent overcomes temptation, and shows restraint in good time via league-based satisficing, that a certain sort of regret tied to a single choice seems in order. In particular, it seems appropriate for the agent to mourn the loss of the forgone good that she deprived herself of (e.g., just one more experience of culinary delight) and that she could have had without sacrificing a preferred or incomparable good. Such regret is compatible with fully endorsing one's prior choice and speaks against the idea that, in continued endorsement cases, an agent's mourning the loss of a forgone good must be tied to the idea that the forgone good is no better than the achieved good but is also not fully made up for by the achieved good because the goods are (too) different in kind.

The key take-home messages of this book can be roughly captured as follows: Challenging choice situations can prompt disorderly preferences, even among rational agents. The subjective appraisal responses instrumental rationality is accountable to will thus not always be neat. Fortunately, rationality can handle quite a lot of messiness. This is important, since rationality wouldn't be all that helpful if, whenever messiness threatened, we had to rush to its rescue rather than look to it for guidance.

References

Ahmed, A. 2014. Comment feed (02/26/14–02/28/14) on "The Self-Torturer and Instrumental Rationality" (02/26/14). *PEA Soup: Philosophy, Ethics, Academia*, http://peasoup.typepad.com/peasoup/2014/02/the-selftorturer-and-instrumental-rationality.html#more.

Ainslie, G. 2001. *Breakdown of Will*. Cambridge: Cambridge University Press.

Aldred, J. 2007. "Intransitivity and Vague Preferences." *Journal of Ethics* 11: 377–403.

Anand, P. 1993. "The Philosophy of Intransitive Preference." *The Economic Journal* 103: 337–346.

Andreou, C. 2005. "Incommensurable Alternatives and Rational Choice." *Ratio* 18: 249–261.

Andreou, C. 2006a. "Environmental Damage and the Puzzle of the Self-Torturer." *Philosophy & Public Affairs* 34: 95–108.

Andreou, C. 2006b. "Temptation and Deliberation." *Philosophical Studies* 131: 583–606.

Andreou, C. 2007a. "There Are Preferences and Then There Are Preferences." In *Economics and the Mind*, edited by B. Montero and M. D. White, 115–126. London: Routledge.

Andreou, C. 2007b. "Environmental Preservation and Second-Order Procrastination." *Philosophy & Public Affairs* 35: 233–248.

Andreou, C. 2010. "Sweating the Small Stuff." *Psychology Today*. https://www.psychologytoday.com/us/blog/choosing-well/201003/sweating-the-small-stuff.

Andreou, C. 2011. "Choosing Well: Value Pluralism and Patterns of Choice." In *New Waves in Ethics*, edited by Thom Brooks, 48–63. New York: Palgrave Macmillan.

Andreou, C. 2012. "Self-Defeating Self-Governance." *Philosophical Issues* 22: 20–34.

Andreou, C. 2014a. "Temptation, Resolutions, and Regret." *Inquiry* 57: 275–292.

Andreou, C. 2014b. "The Good, the Bad, and the Trivial." *Philosophical Studies* 169: 209–225.

Andreou, C. 2015a. "The Real Puzzle of the Self-Torturer: Uncovering A New Dimension of Instrumental Rationality." *Canadian Journal of Philosophy* 45: 562–575.

Andreou, C. 2015b. "Parity, Comparability, and Choice." *Journal of Philosophy* 112: 5–22.

Andreou, C. 2016. "Cashing Out the Money-Pump Argument." *Philosophical Studies* 173: 1451–1455.

Andreou, C. 2017. "Dynamic Choice." In *Stanford Encyclopedia of Philosophy*, edited by E. N. Zalta. http://plato.stanford.edu/archives/spr2017/entries/dynamic-choice/.

Andreou, C. 2019a. "Better Than." *Philosophical Studies* 176: 1621–1638.

Andreou, C. 2019b. "Regret, Sub-optimality, and Vagueness." In *Vagueness and Rationality in Language Use and Cognition*, edited by R. Dietz, 49–59. New York: Springer.

Andreou, C. 2019c. "Can Every Option Be Rationally Impermissible?" *Erkenntnis*. https://doi.org/10.1007/s10670-019-00155-w.

Andreou, C. 2020a. "Empowering Rationality." *American Philosophical Quarterly* 57: 105–115.

Andreou, C. 2020b. "Rationality, Regret, and Choice over Time." In *The Routledge Handbook of Practical Reason*, edited by Ruth Chang and Kurt Sylvan, 505–513. London: Routledge.

Andreou, C. 2020c. "In a Different League: Intransitivity, Betterness, and League-Based Satisficing." In *Derek Parfit's Reasons and Persons*, edited by A. Sauchelli, 117–128. London: Routledge.

Andreou, C. 2021. "Incomparability and the Huge-Improvement Arguments." *American Philosophical Quarterly* 58: 307–318.

Andreou, C. 2022. "Parity without Imprecise Equality." In *Value Incommensurability: Ethics, Risk, and Decision-Making*, edited by H. Andersson and A. Herlitz, 71–83. New York: Routledge.

Andreou, C. Unpublished. "Agency, Options, and Control: Can an Agent Survive on Synchronic Control?"

Andreou, C. Unpublished. "Preferences, Proxies, and Rationality."

Ariely, D. 2008. *Predictably Irrational*. New York: HarperCollins.

Arntzenius, F., and D. McCarthy. 1997. "Self Torture and Group Beneficence." *Erkenntnis* 47: 129–144.

Benbaji, Y. 2009. "Parity, Intransitivity, and a Context-Sensitive Degree Analysis of Gradability." *Australasian Journal of Philosophy* 87: 313–335.

Boot, M. 2017a. "Problems of Incommensurability." *Social Theory and Practice* 43: 313–342.

Boot, M. 2017b. *Incommensurability and Its Implications for Practical Reasoning, Ethics and Justice*. London: Rowman & Littlefield International.

Brandstätter, V., A. Lengfelder, and P. M. Gollwitzer. 2001. "Implementation Intentions and Efficient Action Initiation." *Journal of Personality and Social Psychology* 81: 946–960.

Bratman, M. E. 1999. "Toxin, Temptation, and the Stability of Intention." In *Faces of Intention*, 58–90. Cambridge: Cambridge University Press.

Bratman, M. E. 2003. "A Desire of One's Own." *Journal of Philosophy* 5: 221–242.

Bratman, M. E. 2007. *Structures of Agency*. New York: Oxford University Press.

Bratman, M. E. 2009. "Intention, Practical Rationality, and Self-Governance." *Ethics* 119: 411–443.

Bratman, M. E. 2012. "Time, Rationality and Self-Governance." *Philosophical Issues* 22: 73–88.

Bratman, M. E. 2014. "Temptation and the Agent's Standpoint." *Inquiry* 57: 293–310.

Bratman, M. E. 2018. *Planning, Time, and Self-Governance*. New York: Oxford University Press.

Broome, J. 1993. "Can a Humean Be Moderate?" In *Value, Welfare, and Morality*, edited by R. G. Frey and C. W. Morris, 54–73. Cambridge: Cambridge University Press.

Broome, J. 2000. "Incommensurable Values." In *Well-Being and Morality: Essays in Honour of James Griffin*, edited by R. Crisp and B. Hooker, 21–38. Oxford: Oxford University Press.

Broome, J. 2001. "Are Intentions Reasons? And How Should We Cope with Incommensurable Values?" In *Practical Rationality and Preference*, edited by C. W. Morris and A. Ripstein, 98–120. Cambridge: Cambridge University Press.

Budolfson, M. B. 2018. "The Inefficacy Objection to Consequentialism and the Problem with the Expected Consequences Response." *Philosophical Studies*. https://doi.org/10.1007/s11098-018-1087-6.

Carlson, E. 1996. "Cyclical Preferences and Rational Choice." *Theoria* 62: 144–160.

Carlson, E. 1997. "The Intrinsic Value of Non-Basic States of Affairs." *Philosophical Studies* 85: 95–107.

Carlson, E. 2011a. "The Small-Improvement Argument Rescued." *Philosophical Quarterly* 61: 171–174.

Carlson, E. 2011b. "Defining Goodness and Badness in Terms of Betterness Without Negation." In *Descriptive and Normative Approaches to Human Behavior*, edited by E. Dzhafarov and L. Perry, 51–66. New Jersey: World Scientific Publishing Co.

Chang, R. 1997. "Introduction." In *Incommensurability, Incomparability, and Practical Reason*, 1–34. Cambridge, MA: Harvard University Press.

Chang, R. 2002a. "The Possibility of Parity." *Ethics* 112: 659–688.

Chang, R. 2002b. *Making Comparisons Count*. New York: Routledge.

Chang, R. 2017. "Hard Choices." *Journal of the American Philosophical Association* 3: 1–21.

Chappell, R. Y. 2015. "Value Receptacles." *Noûs* 17: 409–421.

Chappell, R. Y. 2016. "Do We Have Vague Projects?" *PEA Soup: Philosophy, Ethics, Academia.* http://www.peasoup.us/2016/08/do-we-have-vague-projects/.

Dancy, J. 1993. *Moral Reasons*. Oxford: Blackwell.

Davidson, D., J. C. C. McKinsey, and P. Suppes. 1955. "Outlines of a Formal Theory of Value, I." *Philosophy of Science* 22: 140–160.

De Sousa, R. 1974. "The Good and the True." *Mind* 84: 534–551.

Dougherty, T. 2014. "A Deluxe Money Pump." *Thought* 3: 21–29.

Espinoza, N. 2009. "Some New Monadic Value Predicates." *American Philosophical Quarterly* 46: 31–37.

Ferrero, L. 2012. "Diachronic Constraints of Practical Rationality." *Philosophical Issues* 22: 144–164.

Frankfurt, H. 1971. "Freedom of the Will and the Concept of a Person." *Journal of Philosophy* 68: 5–20.

Gert, J. 2004. "Value and Parity." *Ethics* 114: 492–510.

Glantz, M. 1999. "Sustainable Development and Creeping Environmental Problems in the Aral Sea Region." In *Creeping Environmental Problems and Sustainable Development in the Aral Sea Basin*, 1–25. Cambridge: Cambridge University Press.

Glover, J. 1975. "It Makes No Difference Whether or Not I Do It." *Proceedings of the Aristotelian Society Supplemental Volume* 49: 171–190.

Goodman, N. 1972. *Problems and Projects*. New York: The Bobbs-Merrill Company.

Griffin, J. 1986. *Well-Being*. Oxford: Oxford University Press.

Gustafsson, J. E. 2013. "The Irrelevance of the Diachronic Money-Pump Argument for Acyclicity." *Journal of Philosophy* 110: 460–464.

Gustafsson, J. E. 2020. "Population Axiology and the Possibility of a Fourth Category of Absolute Value." *Economics and Philosophy* 36: 81–110.

Gustafsson, J., and N. Espinoza. 2010. "Conflicting Reasons in the Small-Improvement Argument." *Philosophical Quarterly* 60: 754–763.

Handfield, T. 2014. "Rational Choice and the Transitivity of Betterness." *Philosophy and Phenomenological Research* 89: 584–604.

Handfield, T., and W. Rabinowicz. 2018) "Incommensurability and Vagueness in Spectrum Arguments: Options for Saving Transitivity of Betterness." *Philosophical Studies* 175: 2373–2387.

Hansson, S. O., and T. Grüne-Yanoff. 2018. "Preferences." In *Stanford Encyclopedia of Philosophy*, edited by E. N. Zalta. https://plato.stanford.edu/archives/sum2018/entries/preferences/.

Holton, R. 2009. *Willing, Wanting, Waiting*. Oxford: Clarendon.

Hsieh, N. 2005. "Equality, Clumpiness and Incomparability." *Utilitas* 17: 180–204.

Hurka, T. 1996. "Monism, Pluralism, and Rational Regret." *Ethics* 106: 555–575.

Hurley, S. 1989. *Natural reasons*. New York: Oxford University Press.

Kagan, S. 2011. "Do I Make a Difference?" *Philosophy & Public Affairs* 39: 105–141.

Kahneman, D., J. L. Knetsch, and R. H. Thaler. 1991. "The Endowment Effect, Loss Aversion, and Status Quo Bias." *Journal of Economic Perspectives* 5: 193–206.

Levi, I. 2002. "Money Pumps and Diachronic Books." *Philosophy of Science* 69: S235–S247.

MacIntosh, D. 2010. "Intransitive Preferences, Vagueness, and the Structure of Procrastination." In *The Thief of Time: Philosophical Essay on Procrastination*, edited by C. Andreou and M. D. White, 68–86. New York: Oxford University Press.

McClennen, E. F. 1990. *Rationality and Dynamic Choice*. New York: Cambridge University Press.

Millgram, E. 2009. "Practical Reasoning for Serial Hyperspecializers." *Philosophical Explorations* 12: 261–278.

Mintoff, J. 1997. "Slote on Rational Dilemmas and Rational Supererogation." *Erkenntnis* 46: 111–126.

Nefsky, J. 2012. "Consequentialism and the Problem of Collective Harm: A Reply to Kagan." *Philosophy & Public Affairs* 39: 364–395.

Nussbaum, M. C. 1986. *The Fragility of Goodness*. Cambridge: Cambridge University Press.

Papineau, D. 2015. "Can We Really See a Million Colours?" In *Phenomenal Qualities*, edited by P. Coates and S. Coleman, 274–297. New York: Oxford University Press.

Parfit, D. 1984. *Reasons and Persons*. Oxford: Oxford University Press.

Pollock, J. L. 1983. "How Do You Maximize Expectation Value?" *Noûs* 17: 409–421.

Portmore, D. W. 2019. *Opting for the Best: Oughts and Options*. New York: Oxford University Press.

Qizilbash, M. 2018. "On Parity and the Intuition of Neutrality." *Economics and Philosophy* 34: 87–108.

Quinn, W. 1993a. "The Puzzle of the Self-Torturer." In *Morality and Action*, edited by P. Foot, 198–209. Cambridge: Cambridge University Press.

Quinn, W. 1993b. "Putting Rationality in its Place." In *Morality and Action*, edited by P. Foot, 228–255. Cambridge: Cambridge University Press.

Rabinowicz, W. 2000. "Money Pump with Foresight." In *Imperceptible Harms and Benefits*, edited by M. J. Almeida, 123–154. Dordrecht, Germany; London, UK: Kluwer Academic.

Rabinowicz, W. 2008. "Value Relations." *Theoria* 74: 18–49.

Rabinowicz, W. 2009. "Incommensurability and Vagueness." *Aristotelian Society Supplementary Volume* 83: 71–94.

Rabinowicz, W. 2012. "Value Relations Revisited." *Economics and Philosophy* 28: 133–164.

Raffman, D. 1994. "Vagueness without Paradox." *Philosophical Review* 103: 41–47.

Raz, J. 1986. *The Morality of Freedom*. Oxford: Clarendon Press.

Regan, D. 1997. "Value, Comparability, and Choice." In *Incommensurability, Incomparability, and Practical Reason*, edited by R. Chang, 129–150. Cambridge, MA: Harvard University Press.

Savage, L. 1972. *The Foundations of Statistics*. New York: Dover Publications.

Schick, F. 1986. "Dutch Bookies and Money Pumps." *Journal of Philosophy* 83: 112–119.

Simon, H. 1955. "A Behavioral Model of Rational Choice." *Quarterly Journal of Economics* 69: 99–118.

Slote, M. 1989. *Beyond Optimizing: A Study of Rational Choice*. Cambridge, MA: Harvard University Press.

Stocker, M. 1990. *Plural and Conflicting Values*. Oxford: Clarendon Press.

Temkin, L. S. 1996. "A Continuum Argument for Intransitivity." *Philosophy & Public Affairs* 25: 175–210.

Temkin, L. S. 2005. "A 'New' Principle of Aggregation." *Philosophical Issues* 15: 218–234.

Temkin, L. S. 2012. *Rethinking the Good*. Oxford: Oxford University Press.

Tenenbaum, S. 2020. *Rational Powers in Action*. Oxford: Oxford University Press.

Tenenbaum, S., and D. Raffman. 2012. "Vague Projects and the Puzzle of the Self-Torturer." *Ethics* 123: 86–112.

Thaler, R. 1980. "Toward a Positive Theory of Consumer Choice." *Journal of Economic Behavior and Organization* 1: 39–60.

Thoma, J. Unpublished. "Preference Cycles and the Requirements of Instrumental Rationality."

Thompson, M. 2008. "Naïve Action Theory." In *Life and Action*, 83–146. Cambridge, MA: Harvard University Press.

Tversky, A., and D. Kahneman. 1974. "Judgment under Uncertainty." *Science* 185: 1124–1130.

Vineberg, S. 2016. "Dutch Book Arguments." In *Stanford Encyclopedia of Philosophy*, edited by E. N. Zalta. https://plato.stanford.edu/archives/spr2016/entries/dutch-book/.

Voorhoeve, A., and K. Binmore. 2006. "Transitivity, the Sorites Paradox, and Similarity-Based Decision-Making." *Erkenntnis* 64: 101–114.

Watson, G. 1975. "Free Agency." *Journal of Philosophy* 72: 205–220.

Watson, G. 1987. "Free Action and Free Will." *Mind* 96: 145–172.

Wegner, D. 2002. *The Illusion of Conscious Will*. London: MIT Press.

Williams, B. 1973. "Ethical Consistency." In *Problems of the Self*, 166–186. Cambridge: Cambridge University Press.

Index

For the benefit of digital users, indexed terms that span two pages (e.g., 52–53) may, on occasion, appear on only one of those pages.